Priorities in Teacher Education

Good teacher education not only enhances the understanding and skills of new teachers, but also increases the likelihood of them staying in the profession. In *Priorities in Teacher Education*, Kosnik and Beck argue that teacher preparation should be given sharper focus, identifying seven priority areas:

- program planning;
- pupil assessment;
- classroom organization and community;
- inclusive education;
- subject content and pedagogy;
- professional identity;
- a vision for teaching.

Long-time teacher education instructors and researchers themselves, the authors identified these priorities through literature-based research and the findings of a three-year study following twenty-two graduates through their first years of teaching. Packed with examples and quotes about these experiences, the book is broken down into seven chapters, each focusing on one of the priorities and containing a case study of one teacher whose experiences embody the priority being discussed.

As the chapters progress, the authors increasingly demonstrate the interplay between the seven priorities, showing that none of them can be pursued in isolation, and building a comprehensive base of essential knowledge for beginning teachers.

Teacher educators will find *Priorities in Teacher Education* a key guide to pre-service preparation, and new and student teachers will benefit enormously from reading the "front line" accounts of their contemporaries.

Clare Kosnik is Associate Professor and Head of the Centre for Teacher Development in the Department of Curriculum, Teaching and Learning at the Ontario Institute for Studies in Education, University of Toronto.

Clive Beck is Professor in the Centre for Teacher Development and the Department of Curriculum, Teaching and Learning at the Ontario Institute for Studies in Education, University of Toronto.

Priorities in Teacher Education

The 7 Key Elements of Pre-Service Preparation

Clare Kosnik and Clive Beck

Routledge
Taylor & Francis Group

LONDON AND NEW YORK

First published 2009
by Routledge
2 Park Square, Milton Park, Abingdon, Oxon, OX14 4RN

Simultaneously published in the USA and Canada
by Routledge
29 West 35th Street, New York, NY 10001

Routledge is an imprint of the Taylor & Francis Group, an informa business

© 2009 Clare Kosnik and Clive Beck

Typeset in Garamond by Prepress Projects Ltd, Perth, UK
Printed and bound in Great Britain by CPI Antony Rowe, Chippenham, Wilts

British Library Cataloguing in Publication Data
A catalogue record for this book is available from the British Library

Library of Congress Cataloging in Publication Data
Kosnik, Clare Madott.
Priorities in teacher education : the 7 key elements of pre-service
preparation / Clare Kosnik and Clive Beck.
p. cm.
Includes bibliographical references.
1. Teachers—Training of. I. Beck, Clive. II. Title.
LB1707.K675 2009
370.71´1—dc22
2008044897

ISBN10: 0–415–48126–0 (hbk)
ISBN10: 0–415–48127–9 (pbk)

ISBN13: 978–0–415–48126–7 (hbk)
ISBN13: 978–0–415–48127–4 (pbk)

To our research team, for their unfailing commitment
to the project, their warmth and sensitivity in
interacting with the new teachers, their invaluable
input and guidance, their sense of humor and
camaraderie, and their willingness to learn
alongside us.

Contents

Preface

Priorities in teacher education

Teacher education plays a crucial role in the preparation of teachers, not only enhancing their understanding and skill but also increasing the likelihood of their staying in the profession (Darling-Hammond, 2000; Roth, 1999). However, several contemporary researchers maintain that teacher preparation could be more effective if it had a sharper focus. They say that we often try to cover too many topics in our programs and as a result cannot deal adequately with priority areas. Hagger and McIntyre (2006) state that in initial teacher education "it is always necessary to be selective, to prioritize." And Darling-Hammond and Bransford (2005) advocate attending to "knowledge deemed essential for beginning teachers"; they go on to highlight "core" areas such as learning, development, assessment, and classroom management.

Obviously, in order to have priorities in teacher education we have to determine what they are, and this is no easy matter. But we believe that with continued research and discussion – building on the work already done – considerable clarity and consensus could be achieved. The main problem has been that we have rarely raised the issue of priorities and so have denied ourselves the chance to address it.

In this book we recommend giving priority to the following seven elements in pre-service preparation:

- program planning
- pupil assessment
- classroom organization and community
- inclusive education
- subject content and pedagogy
- professional identity
- a vision for teaching.

Of course, this list is of little help in itself: much depends on how the various items are interpreted. As the book unfolds, we discuss in detail the nature of these priorities, how they relate to one another, and the rationale underlying them.

We arrived at these priorities in part through analysis of the literature on teaching and teacher education, and in the book we refer often to this literature. In addition, as long-time teacher education instructors and researchers ourselves, we have drawn on our own experiences and observations in a variety of university and school settings. In fact, we have already "tried out" many of our emerging ideas with our pre-service and graduate students, and their feedback has influenced our thinking considerably. The main focus of the book, however, is the findings of a large-scale study we conducted recently of elementary teachers during their first three years of teaching.

Our research study

The setting for the study was our own school of education and a number of surrounding school districts. At the Ontario Institute for Studies in Education in the University of Toronto (OISE/UT), approximately 700 elementary student teachers are enrolled annually in postbaccalaureate programs. Their average age is in the high twenties and many have had considerable career and life experience before beginning their credential program. About 600 enter the one-year B.Ed. program, the remainder enrolling in either the two-year Master of Teaching (M.T.) or the two-year M.A. at the Institute of Child Study. The B.Ed. students are divided among nine cohort programs, each with its own faculty team and a somewhat distinctive emphasis. In a sense, then, there are 11 postbaccalaureate programs in elementary teacher education at OISE/UT.

We began a large-scale research project on our programs in fall 2003, and we plan to continue it into the future. However, the phase of the project we focus on here occurred from 2004 to 2007, when we followed 22 graduates into their first three years of teaching. The participants were those graduates from spring 2004 who obtained elementary teaching positions in fall of that year in Toronto and surrounding areas and who volunteered to take part in the follow-up study. Fortunately, none of the participants dropped out of teaching during the three-year period. The ratio of females (19) to males (3) is a function of who volunteered but is about the same as the ratio typically found across the programs. The new teachers were from five of the programs, including the two master's programs. Almost all are teaching in schools with a highly multi-racial, multi-ethnic student population and a substantial proportion of ESL students; four of the teachers themselves belong to racial minorities and many have parents who were immigrants from non-English speaking countries.

In each of their first two years of teaching, we observed the new teachers in their classroom twice and interviewed them twice. All the interviews were about one hour long and were tape-recorded and transcribed. The first observation and interview occurred mid-way through the year and the second toward the end of the year. In their third year, we selected seven of the teachers for case studies, observing and interviewing them twice; the remainder we observed and interviewed once toward the end of the school year. Over the three years the interview questions were modified somewhat to match the stage in the teachers' experience. In each round of interviewing, the same questions were asked of all participants, but probe questions were also asked and additional comment encouraged. A central focus of the interviews was literacy teaching, and this is reflected in the data. However, we also often asked about teaching other subjects – notably mathematics – and about more general aspects of teaching and teacher education.

Our research approach was qualitative, as defined by Punch (2005). For example, we had a relatively small sample of new teachers (the 22), our interview sessions were largely open-ended, and the themes emerged as the study progressed. In analyzing the transcripts and observation notes, we began by reading them several times to identify themes or "codes" related to the central issues of the study. We then developed a table of these themes matched to participants and, going through the materials again, recorded the pages on which reference was made to each topic; this table was used in establishing frequencies and developing a structure for our findings. As we wrote up the findings for the book we kept going back to the materials for clarification, continuing to add, delete, and modify themes.

The book

In the seven chapters of the book (after the Introduction) we focus in turn on the seven priorities we identified. We begin each chapter with a brief profile of a new teacher whose experiences and approach seem especially relevant to the priority in question. We then go on to discuss the nature and importance of the priority, the challenges it poses, possible ways of meeting the challenges in the school classroom, and how the priority might be addressed in pre-service education. As we go through the chapters we highlight increasingly the links between the priorities, since we believe that none of them can be pursued in isolation. Chapter 6 on professional identity and Chapter 7 on vision are especially important in showing connections.

We include in the book many references to the research literature on teaching and teacher education. However, most of the quotations and examples come from the new teachers we studied. This is partly because we studied them intensively for three years and so gathered a great deal of original data from them. But it is also because, in our experience, education faculty, pre-service students, and in-service teachers find the new teachers' views especially informative and credible, since they are "on the front lines" and their memories of pre-service education are so fresh. Of course, it is important not to accept the opinions of the new teachers uncritically, given how recently they entered the profession. Nevertheless, we were impressed with their insights into the challenges of teaching and how to address them, and feel their views deserve to be widely disseminated and discussed.

Acknowledgements

We wish to thank our study participants for their continuous willingness to be part of the project on which this book is based. Year after year, these 22 new teachers have welcomed us into their classrooms, generously giving their time for interviews, showing great commitment to their pupils, and offering thoughtful comments and suggestions about teaching and teacher education. We acknowledge the strong support of our colleagues, especially Larry Swartz, who provided invaluable assistance with every aspect of the research. Sincere thanks are due to Frances Tolnai, whose exceptionally able transcribing of the interviews was crucial to the effectiveness of the study. Finally, we wish to thank the Social Sciences and Humanities Research Council of Canada for its generous funding of the research.

Introduction

What should our priorities be in teacher education? As indicated in the Preface, that is the central question of this book. However, the search for priorities raises the further question: why is it important to have priorities? What is the harm in having teacher educators "cover the waterfront" or, alternatively, follow their particular concerns and passions, leaving it up to teacher candidates themselves to choose their approach to teaching? In this introduction we begin by explaining why we believe the widespread lack of prioritization in teacher education is a serious problem, requiring urgent attention. We then give a sample of new teacher views on the topic, followed by some general principles for addressing priorities in a pre-service program.

Lack of direction in teacher education

In a sense, new teachers today receive a great deal of direction on what and how to teach. Their pre-service instructors offer them a wide array of theories, principles, and strategies, and their practicum mentors give them plenty of practical advice. After graduating, they are handed detailed curriculum guidelines, prescribed or recommended teaching materials, and mandated assessment and reporting systems. Further guidance usually comes from their school principal, experienced colleagues, and school district and government induction programs. At a less formal level, teachers are also aware of the views of parents, politicians, and the public at large about how they should do their job.

In practice, however, this guidance system breaks down. In the first place, teachers cannot possibly cover all the ground they are asked to, especially in the early stages of their development (Bransford, Darling-Hammond, and LePage, 2005; Hagger and McIntyre, 2006). As a result, they alternate between a firm resolve to cover everything and half-guilty decisions to omit or de-emphasize certain topics so they have time for other topics they know are crucial. Second, the guidance they receive is frequently inconsistent. Teacher educators' views about what is important vary even within the same preparation program, and these views in turn are often at odds with government and school district policies and practices and parental expectations. As Kennedy (2006) states: "Society holds many lofty aims for education in general and for teaching in particular, but these aims are inconsistent with one another" (p. 206). Third, the ideas presented in teacher education programs tend to be rather abstract, requiring new teachers to figure out for themselves what they mean and how to implement them (Hagger and McIntyre, 2006; Tom, 1997). Along these lines, one of the new teachers in our study said: "I don't think I was clear enough about what a balanced literacy program looks like. I thought I knew and then when I came here I realized I didn't."

Of course, some people might see this as a fortunate situation. It appears to honor academic freedom and give new teachers the opportunity to "construct" their own pedagogy. Some might applaud the fact that, despite the best efforts of teacher educators, school district officials, and government authorities, teachers are left to make many key decisions about their practice. A more concerted and focused approach could easily stifle professional creativity and initiative.

But on the whole we do not share this sanguine view. Certainly, as we argue later, teachers should be free to make many professional choices. However, in teacher education at present, student teachers are neither consistently informed that they have such choice nor adequately prepared to exercise it. As a consequence, when they get their own classroom they are often unable to deal positively with their freedom. Candice, in her first year, commented: "In September, trying to prepare a year, I felt totally lost."

In our experience, even in pre-service programs in which choice by *pupils* is advocated (in the name of constructivism, child-centered pedagogy, and the like), discussion of curriculum selection by *teachers* is not common. Although we stress that pupils should be allowed to follow the path they find most useful and meaningful, we rarely tell teacher candidates that *they* should develop priorities and make choices about what to emphasize. Full coverage of the curriculum by teachers tends to be implicitly endorsed in pre-service programs. Moreover, we often *model* a coverage mentality in pre-service education by trying to touch on almost every aspect of educational theory and practice. Feiman-Nemser (2001) describes some teacher educators as "trying to cram too much into their courses, because they believe this is their last chance to influence prospective teachers" (p. 1016). One teacher educator we interviewed said: "I feel more comfortable giving them a little bit of everything . . . so they don't go out into the system and think, oh gosh, I've never heard of this." Although this may be an extreme example, there is often a tendency in this direction.

What frequently happens (with the best of intentions) in pre-service education is the following. On the one hand, because coverage of educational theory and practice is so extensive it is necessarily superficial, and so student teachers do not gain a clear grasp of what the theories and practices mean. The breadth of coverage militates against depth of understanding. And without sufficient understanding of what is being proposed, the new teachers cannot select, choose, adapt, and integrate in the constructivist manner envisaged.

On the other hand, to the extent that pre-service students *do* understand what is being advocated, their program is so packed with lectures, seminars, assignments, and practicum requirements that they simply lack the time to critique and integrate the various ideas and create their own approach. And they are even busier in the first two or three years after graduation, so the situation does not improve. Maria said of her first teaching term: "The way I describe it is it's like you're treading water and just trying to keep afloat." Of course, new teachers do develop a pedagogy. But they do so largely "on the fly," with a degree of desperation and even trauma, and often with more attention to survival needs than to the "big ideas" their pre-service instructors hoped they would implement (Kennedy, 2005). And some find the experience so overwhelming that they quit teaching and are lost to the profession.

Moving toward priorities in teacher education

What can be done about this situation? As the above analysis suggests, we believe the heart of the problem is lack of prioritization. Accordingly, the solution lies in identifying priorities and giving them special emphasis in pre-service programs, although with considerable opportunity for student teachers to understand the main themes and assess, modify, and integrate them. When teachers emerge from their preparation program they should *already* have a set of "core ideas" (Bransford, Darling-Hammond, and LePage, 2005, p. 3) and a "beginning repertoire" (Feiman-Nemser, 2001, p. 1018): a selective, integrated set of pedagogical ideas and intentions that, to the degree possible for a new teacher, they can name, understand, own, and implement.

A possible danger of this solution, already alluded to, is that it may constrain academic freedom and limit professional initiative. A particular set of priorities may be imposed on student teachers without enough room for disagreement, dialogue, and individual construction. As Kennedy (2006) observes, "we cannot easily separate (a) helping students develop a more complete and productive vision of teaching from (b) proselytizing, a process that is unbecoming in a university" (p. 209).

However, our response to this concern is twofold. First, a wide-ranging "coverage" approach to pre-service education already limits academic and professional freedom; to think of it as an ideal way to promote free choice and the construction of pedagogy is to delude ourselves. When student

teachers are constantly bombarded with ideas that they have little opportunity to question, they are likely to absorb them uncritically (to the extent
that they grasp them at all). Second, the alternative to a coverage approach
does not have to be inculcation or proselytization. Rather, a coherent, prioritized vision for teaching can be developed *with* student teachers.

Instead of a "we cover, they select and apply" model of teacher education, we propose a "together we figure out" model. This is in keeping with
the interactive inquiry approach to construction of pedagogy advocated
by many theorists in recent times (Beck and Kosnik, 2006; Richardson,
1997). We teacher educators certainly must be forthright in saying what
we think about educational priorities, otherwise student teachers will be
deprived of crucial expert input. But equally we must establish a highly
respectful, dialogical culture in the pre-service program so student teachers
can critique our suggestions and develop their own distinctive approach,
while also helping us modify and refine *our* views. In particular, we need to
learn to speak less in class so there is time for the student teachers' voices
to be heard. "Wait-time" is as important in pre-service instruction as in the
school classroom.

To a degree, the emphasis on prioritization we are advocating is already
present in the literature on teacher education, and increasingly so. Goodlad
(1990) notes that pre-service programs are often so fragmented that student teachers are reduced to "filling a large handbag with discrete bits and
pieces of know-how" (p. 225). He maintains that teacher education must be
guided by a clear concept of teaching and learning (Goodlad, 1994). Tom
(1997) similarly decries the fact that teacher education typically involves
"detailed study of a myriad topics" (p. 213). He calls for integration of
moral and subject matter issues with questions of technique within "the
broadened concept of pedagogy that is so critically important to beginning
teachers" (p. 215). Floden and Buchmann (1990) argue for a "coherent"
teacher education program that helps student teachers acquire a "web of
beliefs." Without such coherence, teachers may be unable to build on what
they learned or even recall what it was (p. 313). More recently (as noted in
the Preface), several teacher education theorists have made the case that,
rather than trying to cover a wide range of topics, teacher educators should
address in depth certain key aspects of teaching (Bransford, Darling-Hammond, and LePage, 2005; Darling-Hammond, 2006; Darling-Hammond
and Bransford, 2005; Feiman-Nemser, 2001; Grossman and Schoenfeld,
2005; Hagger and McIntyre, 2006; Maloch et al., 2003; Shulman, 2004;
Wilson, Floden, and Ferrini-Mundy, 2001). What we are attempting to do
in this book, then, is extend and refine an emerging conception of prioritized teacher education.

In keeping with our belief in dialogical inquiry, the proposals we make
for priorities in teacher education are just that: proposals. They are grist
for the mill of readers, and we see ourselves as open to modifying our ideas

in light of ongoing discussion with teacher educators, student teachers, and teachers. Our goal is not to settle the issue of what is important but rather to support the shift away from overly broad and superficial treatment and toward addressing a set of priorities in depth. In order to do this, however, we believe it is important to present specific priorities for readers to react to, instead of just discussing the issue in general.

What are the sources of our proposals about priorities? As experienced instructors and researchers in pre-service education we have many opinions about what is important, and these of course are reflected in the priorities advocated here. We have also drawn heavily on relevant literature on teaching and teacher education. But above all, as mentioned in the Preface, we have been influenced by a study we conducted recently of teacher education graduates over their first three years of teaching. In what follows, we constantly refer to the findings of this research and quote (using pseudonyms) from the interview transcripts.

New teachers' concerns about their pre-service education

To give an early flavor of the new teachers' views, we present in this section a few examples of what they said was missing from their pre-service preparation. In the remainder of the book we provide a more systematic and positive account of their ideas and practices. It is important to note that the great majority of them thought their pre-service preparation was at least fairly valuable and many were quite enthusiastic about it. The data give no basis for a generally negative assessment of their programs. However, certain concerns came up repeatedly and were often stated in rather strong terms.

For example, although most of the study participants identified theoretical understanding as important to them (contrary to a common stereotype of new teachers), many felt the theory presented in their pre-service program was not explained clearly enough: they were often unable to understand what was being said. Karen commented:

> Some of the time when I was in classes, the language used, the terminology, I didn't know what it meant. Like something as simple as phonics – I know this sounds ridiculous – I didn't know what it meant.

One of the terms often mentioned in this regard was "balanced literacy," which was stressed in all the programs. For example, Vera said that "the things I'm learning about balanced literacy through PD [professional development, *since* graduating] have fleshed out what was just glanced over in the pre-service program." Another key concept many thought was not clearly explained was "guided reading," again a strong emphasis in the programs. Felicity, who was in a two-year program, observed: "With regard to the whole guided reading, balanced literacy approach . . . the pre-service faculty did not prepare us for what that means, what it looks like, and the scheduling of it. I found it very hazy." Anna in her third year noted: "I still don't really know what guided reading is."

Apart from lack of clarity, many of the interviewees felt the theory in their pre-service program was not explored in sufficient *depth*. According to Wanda, "a big hole in terms of the pre-service program [was] that we had a certain amount of theory . . . you touch on the basics [but] you don't really get in and sink your teeth into the whole idea." Liane stated that one of her literacy courses was "utterly lacking in theory and it drove me crazy, to be perfectly honest . . . . Debates were discouraged, seminar style was not happening." Vera in February of her first year said that, after attending some workshops and visiting "exemplary classrooms" as part of her school district induction program, she could now "go a lot deeper into, for example, what does shared reading actually look like, as opposed to just being told, you ought to do shared reading, read about it, and go do it." Paul reported: "Certainly we talked about assessment quite a bit but maybe it wasn't in enough depth, maybe it was too much lip service because they had to talk about it."

The new teachers often associated lack of theoretical clarity and depth in their program with failure to link theory to practice. Many said there needed to be fuller indication of the practical implications of a given concept, principle, or strategy. According to Anna, there should be "more focus on how to do literature circles, like not just the importance of it and the different roles but showing a literature circle in action." Felicity remarked:

> We didn't really learn about guided reading in the program, so I end up in a school that requires it and suddenly have to figure out how to implement it, how to mark the exemplars, the scheduling, rotation of the students, and exactly how to do guided reading [with a small group], because there is an art to it.

She commented further: "I think looking at theory, the theoretical aspect of literacy, is great. But . . . we should have been given actual schedules, examples of how to organize your literacy program . . . so perhaps more observing is needed, more modeling, instead of just a lecturing environment." David said: "I knew what shared reading and guided reading were, and that those have to be done . . . I just would have liked more perspective on what it was like to do that in the classroom."

Apart from the general need for fuller theoretical preparation and linking theory with practice, the new teachers mentioned specific priority areas they thought were not stressed enough in their pre-service program. For example, many felt program planning should have received more attention. According to Tanya, "in the pre-service program they talked about doing and trying a lot of different things, but they didn't suggest a particular type of structure or format." Liane observed: "I definitely could have used more assistance [from pre-service] in developing balanced programs over long periods of time." Anita in her third year commented:

> I wish I'd started out with [backwards planning]. We learned the idea of backwards planning [in the pre-service program] but I wish I'd learned that it's the big ideas that matter and being able to recognize those in the content.

Jeannie, also in her third year, said: "[When I left the program] I knew literacy was important . . . but I didn't have a good idea of the big picture . . . how to get the kids to progress throughout the year and how exactly to set it up."

Pupil assessment was a further aspect of teaching identified as requiring fuller treatment. Marisa remarked that "assessment is this huge thing that is not covered enough [in pre-service] . . . [We needed to] look critically at some actual students' work and assess it." Some of the interviewees said they lacked understanding of the nature and purpose of assessment. For example, John reported:

> Coming in, I really didn't know what I should assess, what I should be looking for . . . I've kind of educated myself on it through reading and asking others. But I really think it should have been covered more . . . why do we do it, and what is it important to look for.

Jody, who was generally very positive about her two-year graduate program, said: "The only thing [I didn't feel prepared in] was assessment; we needed to look at it in a little more detail: running records, DRAs [developmental reading assessments], and the different assessment tools."

Another area many of the new teachers regarded as crucial but in which they felt unprepared was group work (and classroom organization generally). All the pre-service programs emphasize collaborative learning and portray use of guided reading groups as state of the art in literacy teaching. Not surprisingly, then, all the new teachers had been attempting to implement group work in literacy (as well as other subjects). But a recurring theme in the interviews was the almost insurmountable challenge of keeping all the groups and individual students productively on task. For example, Marisa said:

> [T]here was a large focus on centers [in pre-service]; [but] it's so hard to do and it's just so time-consuming and there's so much work involved . . . . It's overwhelming at first to get started because it takes so much time to get the task cards ready and actually think of activities.

To summarize, the new teachers in our study were concerned that certain key areas of teaching were not dealt with adequately in their preparation program. Although several noted that one cannot cover everything in pre-service, they felt that some matters should have been addressed more fully, or at least more effectively. Many of the concerns of the new teachers were in a sense rather practical, and might be interpreted as showing undue preoccupation with immediate survival. However, as the interviews indicated, the teachers had a genuine interest in theory, and in the learning and well-being of their students. Their main reason for wanting to solve the practical problems was so their students could have a richer educational experience. Accordingly, we believe we should not dismiss their concerns as the passing worries of novice teachers.

Some areas that we and other teacher educators see as crucial were not discussed very fully by the study participants. For example, they did not say as much as we might like about subject knowledge, social justice issues, and links to the home and local community. However, they appeared to us to have many important insights into priorities for teaching and teacher education. They also had an admirable *sense* of priorities: they spoke often – especially by the third year – about the need to be selective and focus on the "big ideas," the concepts and skills that will be important to students in the long run. In our view, although we need to assess and supplement their advice, we have much to learn from these teachers about what should be emphasized in teacher preparation programs.

How to address priorities in teacher education

Based on the new teachers' views and other sources, we arrived at the following seven priorities for teacher education (as noted in the Preface):

- program planning
- pupil assessment
- classroom organization and community
- inclusive education
- subject content and pedagogy
- professional identity
- a vision for teaching.

We elaborate on these in turn in the seven chapters of the book. These are not of course the only matters to be attended to in teacher education, but we believe they deserve pride of place.

It is not sufficient, however, to have sound priorities in teacher education; we must also address them appropriately. In our recent text *Innovations in Teacher Education* (Beck and Kosnik, 2006), we have spoken at length about how to implement a pre-service program, and we here briefly review some of the main principles in relation to the priorities. In each of the chapters that follow, we apply these principles (and others) to the priority that is the focus of the chapter.

Integrating the pre-service program to show the connections between priorities

Fragmentation is a longstanding problem in pre-service education, due partly to separation between the subdisciplines of education but also to the way pre-service programs are structured. As Feiman-Nemser (2001) observes: "The typical pre-service program is a collection of unrelated courses and field experiences" (p. 1049). This fragmentation greatly hinders student teachers in understanding the key elements of teaching and weaving them together into a coherent pedagogical approach. For a pre-service program to be effective, the various faculty, supervisors, and mentor teachers must work together – and with the student teachers – to refine and integrate the priorities of teaching.

An important aspect of integrating priorities is addressing the even more basic principles that underlie them. As we discuss in Chapter 7, our vision for teaching is based on certain fundamental principles, notably an inquiry approach to teaching; student construction of knowledge; interactive or reciprocal teaching; and individualization of teaching. By themselves, these principles are too abstract to be useful to educators: a more concrete level of discussion is needed, as for example in the priorities we have presented. However, reference to basic principles that cut across the priorities can help student teachers understand the nature and importance of the priorities and the connections between them. For example, we can discuss how individualization of pupil assessment is necessary so teachers get to know their students, thus enabling them in turn to individualize program planning; and how individualized programming supports inclusive education and student engagement, inquiry, and co-construction of knowledge.

Linking theory with practice, again to make the priorities intelligible

Many of the priorities we have mentioned were in fact addressed to a significant degree in our pre-service programs, but the graduates still did not understand them very clearly. As we saw in the previous section, part of the problem was that the implications of the theory for practice were not explored adequately in pre-service. As teacher educators we must resist the tendency, unfortunately reinforced by the university reward system, to view ourselves primarily as theorists in specialist areas, leaving practice to be addressed by others or figured out by student teachers on their own. Theory and practice are inextricably connected: if we are not familiar with practical realities, we are ill-equipped to develop sound theory or teach it to others. And certainly recent graduates, grappling with the challenges of beginning teaching, are not in a good position to figure out the implications of theory, especially if they barely understood it in the first place.

Embodying the priorities in the teacher education program itself

Both on the university campus and in practicum placements, the key elements of teaching must be illustrated in the way the pre-service program is conducted. If this is not the case, the student teachers again will have difficulty understanding what we are advocating, and they will also wonder whether we really believe it ourselves. For example, we have to embody in the program the approach to student assessment, class community, and inclusive education we are advocating. Apart from the reasons mentioned, showing as well as telling is necessary so we have time to address priority areas in the meager one or two years of a pre-service program.

Of course, no matter how carefully we plan and teach in a pre-service program, we are bound to fail to some degree. In studying graduates of our own program we have been amazed at times at what they "did not hear." We wonder where they (or their minds) were when we explained a particular concept or strategy so clearly, in such detail, and with so many practical examples! This is a common phenomenon in teacher education and is due in part to the difficulty student teachers have learning about teaching before they become "real" teachers with their own classroom. As Maria said, she could not learn certain things in pre-service because she lacked a "context" in which to understand them. Similarly, Vera described how she had difficulty applying what she had learned about assessment:

> I think the assessment piece is really key: knowing how to get at the students' learning and how to take the next step . . . And I think I recall being shown all this [in my pre-service program] and being talked to about it; and I do believe that in my program there was a very balanced literacy focus. But it's just that for some reason, in your first year you are so overwhelmed that you don't remember or think about it or it's not fresh in your mind.

However, we do not believe that the challenges of preparing student teachers justify either throwing up our hands in despair or simply continuing with business as usual. *Much can be done at the pre-service stage*, as many exemplary programs have shown (Beck and Kosnik, 2006). We need to inquire further into which elements of teaching are of most importance for beginning teachers and develop instructional strategies that increase preparedness in these areas. Hammerness, Darling-Hammond, and Bransford

(2005) comment that "the metacognitive elements that are involved in the development of expertise can be developed in teacher education, enabling more teachers to reach . . . strong competence . . . earlier than might otherwise be the case" (p. 380). Further, they cite studies suggesting that "under the right circumstances, with particular kinds of learning experiences, new teachers can develop a more expert practice even as beginning practitioners" (p. 381). Learning to teach is a difficult and never-ending task; but a pre-service program that is prioritized, integrated, and connected to practice – and that embodies its own priorities – can significantly enhance teachers' effectiveness in their initial years and beyond.

Chapter 1

Program planning

The aspect of teaching that emerged in our study as the top priority for teacher education was program planning, that is, creating a program of educational experiences for a class across the whole school year. Student teachers need to learn how to develop a set of topics and activities that are feasible, fit together, engage pupils, and promote deep and important learning. This is sometimes called *program development* or *program design*, but we prefer the term *program planning* because it points to the need for prioritization and time allocation in teaching.

In their first year, teachers are surprised at how little time they have for actual instruction. During pre-service practicums, time was given to them so they could carry out the teaching performances on which they were assessed. Accordingly, they tend to imagine that teaching will be a matter of conducting such performances throughout the year until the whole curriculum has been covered in the subject(s) for which they are responsible. The reality, however, is that teaching time is greatly reduced by interruptions, class cancellations, managing behavior, community building, assessing, reporting, and various other activities, and so they cannot possibly cover all curriculum topics in significant depth. They quickly see that a major dimension of their role is deciding which topics to emphasize and how to fit them together to maximize learning in the time available.

Of course, pre-service education already addresses program planning to a degree: unit and lesson planning are standard topics, along with what should be taught in particular subjects and across subjects. However, the issue of time constraints and prioritization of topics receives little attention. All 22 of our study participants came away from pre-service without an understanding the extent of the planning task or how to go about it. For example, Liane commented:

> The technical literacy elements that I learned [in pre-service] underpin everything I do. However, I needed some way to bring those items together so I could see the larger picture . . . I knew a number of strategies that would be useful to me. But tying it all together . . . was lacking.

Part of the problem here is that it is difficult to understand program planning until one is a "real" teacher with one's own class and a sense of all the responsibilities involved (Jacklin, Griffiths, and Robinson, 2006). However, we believe much more could be done during pre-service to foster such understanding. We can ensure that many key principles and strategies of program planning – above all, selection and prioritization – become part of our student teachers' vision and practice. But this in turn requires that we teacher educators develop clearer and more concrete ideas in this area. Too often our instruction in programming remains at a rather abstract and idealistic level, and we fail to take a stand on some of the difficult choices that must be made (Kennedy, 2006).

Over their first three years, the new teachers in our study reached significant insights into program planning and we detail many of these as the chapter unfolds. We do not wish to suggest that all the teachers achieved all these insights to a high degree: that would be unlikely given their early career stage. Rather, we have used input from the group as a whole (along with ideas from other sources) to form a composite picture of program planning. By way of introduction we present the case of Tanya, who seemed to us to have especially instructive views and practices in this area.

Tanya

As a third-year teacher, life is getting a lot easier. Life is getting a lot like life; I'm getting a life. I'm staying up until 9:00 o'clock at night, which is a huge feat for me because in my first year it was 7:30 and I was falling asleep at the table.

Background

Tanya, a new teacher in her mid-twenties, graduated in 2004 from a two-year master's credential program, specializing in kindergarten through grade 6. Her first three years of teaching, although they went relatively smoothly, were in three different grades – 1, 4, and 3 – in two different schools. The schools, both in the same district, were suburban and fairly affluent and had a high proportion of minority students from South-East Asia and the Middle East, with a small percentage of English Language Learners (ELLs). During the master's program, Tanya had done three of her four practice teaching placements in the school where she was first hired to teach. She felt the extended time in the school was an apprenticeship of sorts. Her associate teachers had been outstanding practitioners and mentors for her.

Tanya's previous undergraduate degree was a Bachelor of Science in child studies. Although not giving her a teaching credential, this small, prestigious program had a teacher preparation component, thus allowing her to begin learning the skills of program planning early in her studies. In the third year of the degree Tanya had two practicum placements, one in a daycare center and one in senior kindergarten. In the fourth year she did a semester-long placement (five days a week) in a grade 2 class, where she could observe and participate in the development and implementation of curriculum units. She thoroughly enjoyed the child studies degree because she acquired a deep understanding of child development, had extended experience working with children, learned skills of curriculum development, and honed her reflective practice skills. During the program, Tanya worked for three summers in a highly progressive daycare center emphasizing inquiry-based learning for both children and staff: the influence of this experience is evident in her current approach to program planning.

Tanya was very pleased with the master's credential program that followed because it provided opportunities to learn planning and teaching skills while also addressing many theoretical concepts. The literacy courses in particular "gave us the philosophy we needed to make our way through our first year." She elaborated:

> If you come into teaching with the philosophy you want, then the other stuff will follow and you'll figure out how to fit your school's resources into your philosophy. If you have a strong philosophy – like fostering love of reading – that you're just not willing to let go, then you'll figure out the rest.

She recalled that the program also exposed her to a variety of resource materials that helped her in her planning as a beginning teacher.

Description of practice

We consider Tanya's program planning in literacy to be exceptionally strong, especially for a new teacher. Now teaching grade 3, she uses a variety of excellent books of various genres; the reading materials are developmentally appropriate; she links reading and writing; she spends time getting to know her students and carefully tracking their progress; she is highly focused on pupil learning, while recognizing however that children have to be motivated to read and write; she uses oral language as a bridge to print; she integrates literacy skills into the content areas; students read and write for extended periods each day; decoding and comprehension skills are taught both separately and in content-area lessons; and she uses many different teaching techniques (e.g., Readers' Theater, mini-chalk boards, guided reading, literacy centers, and children word processing on their own).

Tanya's skills in program planning evolved over her first three years of teaching, but she was already quite able in her first year. She began in the same school and at the same grade level (grade 1) as in her final master's practicum, with a mentor teacher whose style and philosophy closely matched hers; accordingly, she was able to base her program on the one she had experienced. The mentor teacher did not rely heavily on a formal reading program; rather, she carefully selected texts and lessons from a range of sources. Tanya continued this thoughtful approach to planning, shunning the basal readers in favor of high-quality children's literature and drawing on research to select specific decoding and comprehension skills to teach. By the end of her third year, she was able to report that "my kids are happy. And I feel pretty confident that they feel okay in here. They're willing to take risks, they're learning, they're progressing, and I'm confident they'll do okay next year."

No doubt Tanya's outstanding practicums helped prepare her for the difficult task of program planning; however, this tells only part of the story. As a beginning teacher, Tanya had a clear vision for her literacy program. Toward the end of her first year she said:

> I want the children to become motivated to read and write. I want them to work in a group so they can talk about reading and writing and actually do it, responding to books through writing or more reading, or manipulating something or listening to something rather than answering a question on a worksheet.

Her vision helped guide her selection of topics and tasks; however, she faced programming challenges in her first year, including "knowing how much work to put in front of the students to keep their attention . . . knowing what to teach them and when to teach them and how to teach them." As time passed and she got to know her students better, these challenges decreased significantly.

In each of her first three years Tanya was keen to co-plan with her grade partners, but she had limited success on account of timetabling logistics, conflicting philosophies, and other factors. When teaching grade 4 (in her second year), she and another new teacher co-planned many of their lessons and units and she found this very rewarding and useful.

> We bounce ideas off each other, we have the same books for our literature circles or sometimes we'll split them up and say, You use these ones this round and we'll switch next round. So all that is co-planned and the work is split up, which is very helpful.

However, the mentor formally assigned to her for this second year was teaching a special needs class and had never taught grade 4, thus limiting how much she could assist Tanya with program planning.

Tanya found planning for the older students challenging because "the program in grade 4 is much more driven by [government] curriculum expectations than it was in grade 1." But in general over the three years she became less confined by the formal curriculum because she

> learned how to read between the lines of the curriculum expectations. I've become better at saying, Okay, I know how that would look. When I first started, I'd read the expectation and only think of the expectation in one way – literally, that means they need to do this. Whereas I now see a variety of different ways of realizing the expectation.

One feature of Tanya's planning is her reluctance to use ability groups. She tends to form groups that are heterogeneous and changes them frequently. "I find that if I do ability groups my lower students get lost. And they're the ones I need not to be lost, they're the ones I need to be engaged." She now uses group work extensively, particularly in the literacy centers. Many teachers, especially beginning teachers, find group work problematic because of classroom management issues. In Tanya's philosophy of education, fostering a strong class community is essential if she is going to realize her vision of interactive learning. She spends an enormous amount of time in the first semester of each year building community, teaching social skills, playing non-competitive games during the Daily Physical Activity period, teaching students how to work in groups, developing a respectful culture, and establishing routines. As described below, her students truly work well together.

Tanya's class in action

Tanya's grade 3 classroom (in her third year) is a fairly large, bright room. The tables are arranged in groups and every inch of space is utilized. There are bins of books, crates of art supplies, baggies for the literacy centers, math manipulatives, photographs, books on display, samples of work, word walls reflecting the current units, motivational posters (that are changed regularly), a computer, and a teacher's desk tucked in the corner. The room is colorful and inviting.

One day when we observed Tanya's class, the complexity of her program was evident. The afternoon began with students presenting a Toy Expo. The science expectations for the term were force and movement, both fairly abstract concepts; however, the children had built toys embodying the concepts, using boxes, pipe cleaners, magnets, paper clips, elastics, springs, and so on. Each toy had to illustrate at least one force and one form of movement. The pupils wrote advertisements for their toys using the skills of persuasive writing they had learned in writing class. Another grade 3 class visited the Toy Expo and the scene was a true celebration of learning. The children were thrilled with their toys and could use scientific language to explain how they built them and how they worked.

The Toy Expo was followed by work at the literacy centers. The six centers were: persuasive writing (responding to the text *Click, Clack, Moo, Cows that Type*); making words; listening (story on tape); reading comprehension (each student had an individually chosen book but answered generic questions); team reading; and spelling. There was a quiet hum in the room as the students worked in their centers for 30 minutes. The level of cooperation and time on task was outstanding. The day ended with Tanya reading a chapter from *Jigsaw Joe* and leading pre-reading, during-reading, and post-reading discussion. Throughout the day, she moved among the children giving words of encouragement, asking probing questions, and suggesting strategies. Her approach was caring yet firm.

Ongoing professional learning

During her third year, Tanya remarked that she will spend a lifetime learning how to teach. In every interview she described the many in-service workshops she attended, some focused on content (e.g., literacy) and others on instructional strategies. Both types deepened her vision for her program and strengthened her program planning abilities. By the end of the first semester of the first year she had already attended three after-school workshops on literacy, had numerous meetings with the literacy consultant (all of which she arranged herself), and attended the monthly in-school PD sessions. In the second half of the first year she went to a workshop "almost once a week."

As we have seen, Tanya's talents as a teacher emerged quite quickly. In her second year, the principal asked her to help co-plan a professional development session on instructional strategies. In her third year, she was invited to join several district-level professional development committees, including First Steps and the Schools Attuned Initiative. Participating in committees further increased her confidence and enhanced her own planning and implementation skills.

In conclusion, we can see that Tanya's undergraduate and graduate programs, with their strong academic content and extended practicum placements with able mentors, contributed to her solid formation as a teacher. By the end of her third year, her developed vision for literacy teaching, her deep understanding of child development, her extensive knowledge of balanced literacy, her familiarity with a broad range of curriculum resources, her repertoire of teaching strategies, and her reflective practice were evident in her very effective approach to program planning and teaching generally.

What and why of program planning in the school classroom

Tanya's deep understanding of the need for program planning was unusual for a beginning teacher, being due to distinctive talents and special aspects of her background and training. For most of the new teachers in our study, it came as quite a shock that program planning is such a large part of what teachers do. Like most people, they tended to assume that teachers simply make their way steadily through the mandated curriculum for a given subject and grade. And certainly that is what happens in some countries: all teachers at a particular grade are literally "on the same page" on a given day, teaching the same content and using many of the same activities.

But in the context in which we and our graduates work, much of the responsibility for planning the school day, week, and year lies with the teacher; and this is the case (in varying degrees) in other school systems around the world (Calderhead and Shorrock, 1997; Clayton, 2007; Darling-Hammond, 2006; Hagger and McIntyre, 2006; Kennedy, 2005). Although the official curriculum may list topics and "expectations" for each grade level, the teacher – often guided by broader goals and a deeper vision – decides how closely to follow these guidelines and how to implement them. Even in schools where the principal stresses sticking to the official curriculum, teachers behind their closed door make choices tailored to their class. There are differences of degree, however; teachers vary in how much freedom they think they have and should exercise (Kennedy, 2005; Sleeter, 2005).

With time, all the new teachers in our study came to accept a decision-making role at least to an extent. In April of his first year David said:

> I think I relied too heavily [earlier in the year] on the school board program. It was a security thing for me, to make sure I did what the board asked me to do . . . [I would advise a beginning teacher to think] what do you want to achieve in language arts, what is your language program? If you have a good idea then integrate that with the board program . . . Do yours first and then match it up with the other and don't be afraid to take a little leniency with it. You have to cover the expectations, but don't be afraid to say your activity is covering the expectations just as well as the school board resources are.

Similarly, Nina saw that she had to adapt her program to her students: "I tried to use [an] approach to reading instruction . . . we learned in pre-service, and I think the theory behind it is fantastic, but in a class like mine I simply can't do it."

Briefly put, the program planning role of teachers involves deciding: (a) what topics to include (or how much *emphasis* to place on each topic, if one tries to cover everything on the official list); (b) how to teach the topics: what materials, strategies, and activities to use and what approach to take; (c) at what point in the year to address the topics; and (d) to what extent to integrate the various subjects, topics, and activities. Beyond these choices on particular matters, teachers also decide (e) to what extent and in what ways to pursue broader and deeper learning goals – e.g., love of learning, research skills, collaborative skills, links between learning and everyday life – that cut across topics, activities, and subjects.

Why is so much decision making on the part of the teacher necessary? Indeed, should it be allowed at all? There are several reasons for giving teachers such responsibility. Perhaps the main one is that *learning is unpredictable*: it develops in unforeseen ways and requires different paths for different individuals and groups. Accordingly, although external experts can provide considerable help, learning must be guided by someone who is *on the spot* and knows the students well. For example, Serena in her first year of teaching said that she usually creates her own teaching materials "because in this class, their development is so unpredictable . . . . A lot of stuff I make is very tailored to them . . . knowing what they need." And John described how he sometimes sets aside a planned lesson in order to address "real questions that real children are asking." Such teachable moments can be recognized and capitalized on only by someone in the classroom with decision-making power.

Second, *some topics are more important than others* for given individuals and groups. Teachers need to choose topics and examples that are relevant to the lives of their students, including their family and local community (Barton and Hamilton, 1998; Pahl and Rowsell, 2005). For example, one of the new teachers reported that in trying to make the topic of "medieval times" meaningful for her students, she often departs from traditional content to a degree, giving illustrations from the medieval history of the non-European cultures represented in her class. At a more individual level, children in a class are all attempting to develop and enrich their distinctive *personal* way of life, whatever their cultural background, and so must be allowed to explore topics of particular importance to them (Delpit, 2000; LeCourt, 2004).

Third, program planning by the teacher is necessary because *student engagement is crucial to learning*. All our new teachers came to see this point very clearly. If teachers are given, and exercise, the freedom to choose content and methods of interest to their class, their students will be more involved, will learn in greater depth, and will be less disruptive in class (Allington, 2006; Atwell, 1998; Dewey, 1938). What is engaging to students varies from class to class and student to student and changes over time, and the classroom teacher is typically in the best position to note and act on these variations and changes.

The need for the kind of decision-making and planning role for teachers described above is solidly supported by the literature on teaching and teacher education. For example, according to Dewey (1938),

> [Teaching] requires thought and planning ahead. The educator is responsible for a knowledge of individuals and for a knowledge of subject-matter that will enable activities to be selected which lend themselves to social organization . . . in which all individuals have an opportunity to contribute something.
>
> (p. 56)

Hagger and McIntyre (2006) speak of the importance of the "decisions" teachers make in both the "planning" and "interactive" phases of teaching (pp. 29–30). They state that teaching expertise lies in "very subtle judgments about what standards to set, what actions to take, and what combinations of goals can realistically be sought" (p. 33).

Darling-Hammond (2006) maintains that teachers must have "[t]he capacity to plan instruction so that it meets the needs of students and the demands of content" (p. 95). She refers to teachers as "adaptive experts" with the ability to assess learning difficulties and "adapt materials, teaching strategies, or supports accordingly" (p. 11). She says:

> Teaching that aims at deep learning, not merely coverage of material, requires sophisticated judgment about how and what students are learning, what gaps in their understanding need to be addressed, what experiences will allow them to connect to what they need to know, and what instructional adaptations can ensure that they reach common goals.
>
> (p. 10)

Applying this insight to teacher education, Cappello and Farnan (2006) speak of the need for student teachers to develop "professional judgment" (p. 67), learning to "make instructional decisions as they negotiate national, state, and local accountability measures" (p. 64). They must acquire the capacity to "plan instruction designed to ensure success for a diverse student population" (p. 66).

Problems of program planning in the school classroom

Although seeing the need for program planning was an important start, all our new teachers had difficulty actually doing the planning. An initial challenge was creating the formal "long-range plan" most of them had to submit to their principal within the first few weeks. Anna commented: "I definitely needed to know . . . long-range planning [in September], which I did not know." And Jody said that she "needed to know how to make a long-range plan . . . that was the first thing I had to hand in [to the principal]. And the only reason I sort of knew how to do it was because of a summer institute [I went to]."

In addition to this formal requirement, however, and more importantly, the new teachers did not feel well prepared to develop a working plan for the year: feasible, balanced, integrated, somewhat sequenced, and complete with structures and routines. (They often called this a "long-range plan" too, although it was different from the formal requirement.) In June of her first year, Vera reported: "Long-range planning is still very challenging . . . It's hard to know where I should be and where the students should be at this point in the year." Liane observed:

> I would have preferred . . . a [pre-service] program that helped me learn to structure a balanced literacy program in very specific terms, in terms of long-range planning and that kind of thing, rather than here's a strategy, here's a strategy, here's a strategy. I can open a book and read how to teach students to write a bio-poem, I don't need you to tell me that. I would rather you told me how I could implement that bio-poem idea inside a larger English program that meets the needs of the children . . . I needed more on . . . how to organize my planning for the long-term, planning for balanced literacy, for a variety of skill situations.

As mentioned before, there is a limit to the extent to which student teachers can learn how to do planning of this kind, given they are not yet in a context that involves such responsibilities; but we agree with Liane that more attention needs to be paid to this area in pre-service.

A specific difficulty mentioned by all the interviewees was planning for the wide ability range in their class. Jeannie said that "the biggest challenge is their starting off point . . . some are already reading and some have no letter recognition at all." Anna stated: "It's hard to motivate students who can write very well to write even better when we have to take things slowly for the students who are falling behind . . . It's a challenge for me." According to Candice, "the diversity of student needs was talked about [in the pre-service program] but not the how. There was lots of recognition of the problem, but solutions were lacking." She went on:

> The language program I took last year was awesome . . . [but] I know too much and it paralyzes me . . . Knowing what a perfect program would look like and not being able to put it into action was frustrating: not being able to . . . do all those things at the level at which all the different students need it.

Paul remarked that the pre-service program should have offered "strategies on how to teach a class when you've got 24 students who are all so different and you don't have an EA [educational assistant], it's just *you* . . . [We needed] strategies, even just a sheet of ideas." And David said: "I wasn't prepared for how hard it was to deal with mixed abilities; like it borders on the impossible some days."

Principles and strategies of program planning in the school classroom

So far we have spoken in general terms about the nature, rationale, and challenges of program planning. But if student teachers are to acquire sound concepts and skills in this demanding area, they need detailed suggestions. Although they will soon develop their own approach, one that reflects their distinctive philosophy and context, they require initial input. As Anita said:

> In the pre-service program the instructors didn't want to be prescribing . . . But I would have liked someone to say, "This worked for me, here is one thing you can do, or a variety of things. There are many more out there but you can start with these and then see what works for you." I don't really feel there was enough practical knowledge being passed around.

Fortunately, as time went on, our study participants themselves had much to say about the theory and practice of program planning. Based largely on their comments but also other sources, we outline below a number of principles and strategies we think would be helpful to pre-service students in this area; indeed, we have already begun to share these with our own student teachers.

Recognize the limitations of formal "long-range planning"

As noted, nearly all the new teachers in our study had to submit a "long-range plan" to their principal within a few weeks of beginning to teach. Coming on top of the other pressures of the start-up period, this caused considerable stress. Most had not heard of the requirement before and were not sure what it entailed. They were apprehensive about having to state immediately all their objectives and activities for the year in a document that would be placed on file and for which they thought they would be held accountable.

Student teachers should be helped to understand the limited significance of a formal planning statement of this type. It is typically just a listing of topics from the official curriculum in sequence over the year. It is usually compiled without consideration of the relative importance of topics, the limitations of time, or the actual sequence that will work best. It has some value as a document to show to parents (often in abbreviated form) and to help teachers gain an overview of the official curriculum, but developing it is a very small part of the real task of program planning.

Moreover, as our new teachers later learned, the long-range plan requirement varies considerably from school to school. Principals differ in how comprehensive they expect the plan to be and how much time they give to reading it and checking adherence to it. Variations were also noted in the help available to develop the plan: in some cases new teachers have to create it largely on their own but in others they are given assistance. Maria reported that at her school small groups of teachers do long-range planning "as a team, in all subjects. The only thing we do on our own is how we teach it." David said he "started off with a long-range plan from a teacher who taught this grade last year, who I worked with as a student teacher." Anna commented: "We have a school district resource disk where it's click, copy, and paste . . . It's got everything and every modification."

Obviously, new teachers should find out as quickly as possible the expectations in their school and school district and take advantage of whatever help is given. Above all, they must distinguish between this largely formal requirement and the much more important and demanding task of realistic, substantive planning for instruction in their classroom.

Identify your main goals

Turning to the substance of program planning, a crucial step is to identify your main goals for the year. Time does not permit in-depth coverage of all topics in the official curriculum (although we may touch on all of them to some degree). We must have certain large objectives to which we give priority. This point was made by many of our new teachers, especially in their second and third years. For example, Vera, who was teaching grade 1, said:

> [I]n my first couple of years I would always wonder, Am I doing this right? Is this going to meet the curriculum expectations? . . . But as I move along my concern is becoming, How can I ensure that the kids . . . are able to do the things they have to do, like read different types of materials independently, select appropriate texts on their own, tackle difficult words they come across, comprehend what they're reading? It's these big-picture ideas that I focus on.

Toward the end of her third year teaching grade 4/5, Anita commented:

> We can't possibly cover all the content . . . so we need to look at the big ideas or the main skills the kids require for success in a subject. So I often think about – and write down – what my goals are, what

I'm trying to teach really . . . In literacy, for example, I focused in first term on the planning aspect of writing, how to generate ideas . . . And then in second term, we focused on how to plan and structure an informational report. So again, those big ideas . . . strategies they can use in any writing context.

Nina, teaching grade 2, observed:

The curriculum expectations are for the most part very reasonable . . . But now [at the end of year 3] I realize that, especially in science – which is my background – I should focus on critical thinking. Because two years from now the kids are not going to remember all the vocabulary around motion, and wedges, and these different things. But they will remember how they did their research, how they approached it.

In these quotations, then, the new teachers mentioned the following goals as being key for their students:

- being able to read independently
- selecting appropriate texts on their own
- knowing how to tackle new words
- comprehending what they're reading
- planning and generating ideas for writing
- planning and structuring an information report
- critical thinking
- knowing how to approach research.

The above is just an illustrative list from the quotations presented, and the goals are mainly academic ones. Other types of goals often mentioned by the participants in our study include:

- learning how to converse
- enjoying interaction with peers
- being able to resolve conflicts
- acquiring a sense of equity and inclusion
- developing an idea of what you want to do in life.

We agree with Anita that it is useful to write down our goals as teachers, but we should not see them as fixed. Our interpretation of them will change as our students change and as we gain new insights into what is important. Also, we will keep adding to our list: over the years it will become quite long. At any given time, however, we should focus on a relatively small number of goals, realizing that as we pursue one goal we will promote many others as well. For example, as we teach the purpose of mathematics we will teach about the nature of numbers and how to apply mathematics.

Focusing on a set of goals does not make our teaching narrow, but rather gives a basis for prioritization and integration.

Establish classroom structures that promote learning

Having identified our main goals, a further key step is to create classroom structures and routines that promote these goals almost automatically during the course of the school day. Kennedy (2006) speaks of the need for teachers to have "a collection of ready-made responses . . . practices that are automated enough that they can be sustained without excessive cognitive or emotional burden" (p. 206). According to Cunningham and Allington (2007): "The most effective teachers provide all the important ingredients that go into creating thoughtful, avid readers and writers" (p. 7). Miller (2002) stresses the need to establish a "framework" or "format" for the daily reading workshop that incorporates the key dimensions of learning to read. She argues that a predictable context is not boring to teacher and students but, on the contrary, enables creativity to flourish (pp. 7–8).

Classroom structures of this kind are not only effective in promoting learning; they are essential if teaching is to be manageable. Once we give up the idea that teaching is just working our way through the official curriculum using a textbook that does the same, we appear to be faced with preparing an endless series of lessons from scratch. Establishing classroom learning structures can help us deal with this situation. With many learning activities already in place, much of our lesson planning can take the form of tweaking these activities. This means we are less anxious about whether a particular lesson will work since we have already tried it in some form; and the time we save by this approach frees us to keep adding a smaller number of truly different and exciting lessons and activities. Moreover, students also typically appreciate such structures because they too are doing things they have enjoyed and been successful at in the past.

Many of our study participants stressed the importance of having classroom learning structures. Marisa, who put a great deal of time into lesson preparation, said nevertheless: "Structure helps, especially in the first year, because you know what to do and you don't feel you're picking things out of thin air . . . I find that the more structure I have, the easier it is to plan." Jeannie, after her third year teaching grade 1, described the structure she had in place for literacy instruction:

> Basically, the first hour in the morning was spent on reading and the second hour after recess was on writing. In my reading workshop we always did shared reading, normally a poem: we had a poem of the week with a different focus each day. Then they would go and rotate around the literacy centers while I did my guided reading groups.

For example, there was a word study center focusing on five high-frequency words each week, and a poetry center that involved shared reading of a poem.

The learning structures mentioned by the new teachers included:

- learning centers
- literature circles
- guided reading
- teacher reading to the whole class
- regular independent silent reading
- poem of the week
- word study
- writing scrapbook
- book reports in varied formats
- bell work
- math challenge
- extra activities when work completed early
- Monday morning carpet sharing
- culminating projects in varied formats.

Make use of textbooks and programs

Although we should keep our main goals firmly in mind and select topics and activities carefully, this is not necessarily incompatible with using comprehensive texts and learning programs. Often new teachers come from pre-service feeling they should develop their own units and lessons, or at least draw on a wide variety of sources. A "pick, choose, and create" outlook was very apparent in our study participants in their first year. Heather reported that her resources "come from everywhere . . . the most important skill [I learned in the pre-service program was] how to find resources around you." Nancy said she believed in "using different resources," and Jody remarked: "I do a little bit of everything." However, by the second or third year many of them saw limitations in this approach and favored greater use of sets of learning materials, though still with considerable selection and modification.

Using textbooks and programs can save time in lesson preparation and free us to be more creative in other ways. As Maria commented:

> You might know all these strategies, but how do you teach them? Teachers don't want to waste all their time looking for books . . . You want something that's easy to access, is available, and is related to the curriculum and to what the government says we need to do.

Nancy discussed her use of the language arts program in her school district:

> I'm free to choose what to do in literacy lessons. But what I should be
> covering and evaluating is integrated through the school district docu-
> ments, which in turn are directly linked to the government curriculum,
> so it does a lot of the work for you. And you know what? I'm such a
> new teacher it has helped me realize what is needed in literacy teaching
> . . . I'm more confident having that document by my side.

Use of texts or packages of materials can also provide a basis for worthwhile collaboration with colleagues who are using the same resources. For
example, Vera tended to pick and choose in her first year but in her second year moved to a school where there was a great deal of collaboration,
which in her view enabled her to "plan a lot more effectively." Wanda at
the end of her third year said:

> I'm a big believer in having consistency in a school program, so if
> certain teachers are following, for example, the Lucy Calkins writing
> program then we should all be following it to a certain extent . . . The
> frameworks in terms of our expectations of students should be very
> similar. This doesn't mean that the way we teach has to be the same,
> but there has to be some divisional-type planning . . . And I believe that
> consistency from year to year creates a stronger student, because they
> know the language and feel comfortable with it; and that in turn makes
> them more willing to take risks, rather than going from one teacher
> whose style is very specific to another who is the polar opposite.

Teachers can also grow professionally as a result of using textbooks and
programs, and the teacher manuals that come with them. Along these lines,
Sophia at the end of her third year commented:

> [This year] we have a new Nelson reader that has been pushed a bit
> by the school administration, and they've spent money on it. And I'm
> using it because . . . although I'm very comfortable coming up with my
> own lessons, obviously there are other people out there who have great
> ideas . . . And the reader is good in that it helps you integrate your
> program and it teaches reading strategies at the same time, although I
> put my own spin on some of the strategies, obviously. And I find that
> it addresses all the different kinds of text, some of which I might not
> necessarily have brought into the classroom because I wouldn't have
> had access to them, at their specific level. So that's different from what
> I did last year.

Similarly, Felicity remarked:

I've started using [in year 3] the Lucy Calkins writing program . . . . Because a lot of the problem I was having was it just wasn't clear to me, coming from teachers college, how to run a good writing program. And this program . . . doesn't just teach you about writing and doing a writers' workshop, it just makes sense overall for good teaching.

Be flexible in following your plan and using resources

While having a plan and utilizing texts and programs, however, we need to be flexible. The ultimate purpose of the plan and materials is to promote key learning goals, and this often requires unanticipated moves. We saw earlier how contemporary scholars stress the importance of teachers making "curriculum decisions" (Darling-Hammond, 2006; Hagger and McIntyre, 2006). Schon (1983) famously described how effective practitioners in any field constantly "reflect in action," modifying their plans as they go. In some cases pupils grasp a point very quickly; in others we need to take the instruction further. Sometimes a "teachable moment" arises unexpectedly, leading us to abandon a prepared lesson.

The importance of flexibility in teaching was mentioned explicitly by all the participants in our study. In his first year, Paul reported: "I'm pretty flexible; often I'll have something I'm going to do and it doesn't really feel like the right thing, so at the very last minute I'll change it." Toward the end of his second year, David observed:

Last year . . . I seemed to be driven to get a lesson done within the set time; and then the next day there was a new lesson. And I think that was detrimental, because . . . the students needed more time to develop and reinforce the concepts . . . So [this year] if the lesson didn't get done, it didn't get done; we'd do it the next day and just move forward with that.

Wanda, who liked the idea of having the whole school "on the same page," nevertheless said: "I guess the reality is that there is no perfect program out there, you need to adapt to suit the kids." Felicity, although adopting the Calkins writing program, noted that she feels comfortable saying, "I don't really like the way she's suggesting I do it, so I'm going to do something different within her general structure." And Sophia, although deciding to use the same reader as her colleagues, commented: "I just hope they don't resort to following the reader as an easy way, I hope they show some creativity . . . I've found a way to use the reader and still make learning to read fun."

One question that arises is *to what extent* individual teachers should deviate from the approach and materials chosen by their school or school district. As we have discussed, there are advantages to having a common program in a school; and also teachers must protect themselves from being dismissed as mavericks (or literally dismissed). Some of the new teachers in our study said they kept quiet about their deviations. Others emphasized the need to be diplomatic: David, as we saw, commented that teachers should claim that their activities are in fact "covering the [official] expectations just as well as the school board resources are." Several teachers in their third year mentioned being taken to task by their colleagues for doing things differently, with remarks such as "you make us look bad" or "why would you put so much work into it?"

As we weigh this issue, we should be aware that sometimes teachers have more latitude than we think (although this varies from one country, state, and school district to another). And often in pre-service programs this latitude is not mentioned. Some of our participants commented that so long as their class is under control and the students are learning, the principal does not bother them. Tanya, while underscoring the courage it took, reported taking the position (in her first year): "No, I'm not going to do it. I understand I'm new, but I'm not doing that worksheet or teaching that way. I'm going to do it my own way." She maintained that new teachers should come from their preparation program with the awareness that not everyone teaches in the same way, and feeling "competent in yourself" to teach the way you believe is best. In her third year, while acknowledging the value of having a common teaching approach, Tanya said: "But at the end of the day, I'm pretty stubborn. If the team is going in a direction that I really don't believe is the best for my students, then I diverge." Obviously, teachers should determine as quickly as possible how much divergence is feasible and appropriate in their particular context.

Individualize your program

One type of flexibility, and a key dimension of program planning, is adapting our program to the diverse pupils in our class. This is emphasized by many writers on education, including Cunningham and Allington (2007), Gardner (1999), Peterson and Hittie (2003), and Sleeter (2005). The relevant pupil diversity is not just academic in nature: it also includes differences of interest, ethnicity, race, gender, way of life, and so on (many of which we will discuss in later chapters). Here, however, we focus especially on academic diversity.

Most of the new teachers in our study felt unprepared for the wide range of academic ability in their class, and some said this was their greatest challenge. Wanda observed that even in a regular grade 1 class the academic spread "can be huge," requiring substantial program modification. Felicity, with a split grade 3/4 class, had enormous differences of literacy ability:

I've got students who are reading at grade 1 level and others at grade 6. Some of my students are writing at grade 1 or 2 or not even that – some don't really even write, everything has to be scribed – while others are writing at grade 5. There are just so many different levels.

Although in our view the need is clear, individualizing instruction is only partly accepted in many schools and school systems. It is a matter on which a teacher may have to take a stand, as discussed in the previous section. Paul said at the end of his third year:

The basic thing is that you have to start wherever the students are. And that is a problem because . . . the curriculum assumes that they come to you with the previous year's material learned, but that's never the case with all or even most of the students. So . . . for me the focus is still on what they need as opposed to what I'm supposed to cram in. And I'm becoming more and more a teacher who says, you know what, I know they expect me to do all this stuff, but the reality is that it's not going to get done, so I'm not even going to bother saying I'll do it. I'm going to do what the kids need . . . and if someone wants to take me to task they can, and then I will explain why I'm doing it.

Paul, it should be mentioned, had several students with severe behavioral problems, and just by surviving he effectively won the right to insist on his approach. Teachers in other settings may have to be more careful in speaking about their individualization practices.

It is important to note that individualized instruction does *not* preclude using whole-class learning methods. As we will discuss in Chapter 3, whole-class interaction is very important for community building, and moreover students can help each other and learn from each other. The whole class is a setting in which students can learn about each other's differences and acquire attitudes and skills of appreciation, acceptance, and conflict resolution. Much of the time, then, rather than separating students we should look for whole-class activities in which everyone can contribute, though in distinctive ways.

Along these lines, a practice advocated by many of our study participants was to teach in a manner that acknowledges the different learning styles and "multiple intelligences" of students in the class (Gardner, 1999). For example, Sophia uses "graphic organizers, charts, and a language-rich environment with labels and words everywhere and color coding." Carrie, teaching grade 8 in her second year, reported:

I try to make sure different learning styles get addressed – visual, oral, and so on; for example in studying Romeo and Juliet they worked in pairs to do a comic strip of a particular act, which they loved; they had to do a time-line, read the act again, and make decisions about what was happening, how to make a picture of it, and how to translate Shakespearean words into present-day English. More generally, I write things on the board, give oral instructions, and have open-ended activities. I try to make sure there's an access point for all of them.

Two of the new teachers gave examples of particular *programs* that are useful in meeting individual needs in a whole-class setting: Calkins's process writing approach, which can be "very tailored and specific" to what a particular child can do; and a spelling program that worked well for weaker spellers but included challenging additional tasks for more able spellers. Finally, several study participants reported providing "accommodations" – such as easier tasks and longer time for completion – for lower-performing students. This complicates marking and reporting, as some noted, but has the advantage of enabling all students to participate with their peers and so feel part of the class community.

Although whole-class teaching is very important, many of the new teachers also advocated giving one-on-one attention to students. For example, Nina said: "[In the past] I focused too much on group work . . . I should have spent more individual time with the children, because their needs are just so different . . . So I plan this last term to do more one-on-one work with students." Nina wondered about the legitimacy of spending more time with less able students, "sometimes to the detriment of the higher students," but in the end felt that students who are struggling because of lack of support at home deserve special help. In the same vein, Marisa commented:

> I think we need to know our students, what kind of home life they have, what experiences they bring with them, and meet them at that point. There's a tendency to blame parents . . . But . . . if I have a parent who's not really helping their child, making them do their homework and stay organized, then I need to come up with a way to help that child stay organized, do their work, and so on . . . as opposed to just saying there's nothing I can do.

There are limits, of course, to the amount of individual attention teachers can give, so other strategies (apart from the whole-class methods noted above) are needed. Wanda said that learning centers where students can work at their own pace and in their own way are often beneficial to struggling learners in the lower grades. She also recommended enlisting the help of children's parents: "This year I've had a couple of struggling students whose parents have definitely been willing to sit down and listen and provide support." Use of pairing and a buddy system within the class were also found to be effective. Felicity said that she pairs lower-ability students with "a higher-ability student who they get along with and who they can ask questions of." Sophia, who had eight special needs students and three ELL students in her grade 4 class, reported:

> I have a peer buddy system in this classroom . . . and each peer buddy assists another student in their group . . . so they can continue learning when I'm not able to get to them. I pick those students because they have fantastic social skills and are willing and able to help; and it's not affecting their performance, in fact it empowers them and they love it.

Integrate your program

A vital aspect of planning a strong program is to integrate it as much as possible, both within subjects and across subjects (Allington, 2006; Meier, 1995; Wood, 1992). We saw a substantial increase in program integration by our study participants over their first three years. As they became more relaxed and got to know the content better, they found ways to link topics, units, and subjects more closely. One reason given for integration was to save time. Paul said that by "integrating math, science, and language into one unit you will cover a lot of things in less time." Sophia observed, "I have integrated more this year [year 3] . . . because . . . I want to address as much of the curriculum as possible." Anita proposed saving time *within* the literacy program by integrating spelling into other language activities, supplemented by mini-lessons as needed. There was considerable disagreement among the new teachers about how far to go in incorporating study of "basic skills" – spelling, phonics, grammar, etc. – into the rest of the curriculum; however, integration was a major emphasis.

Apart from saving time, many of the teachers spoke of integration as a means of increasing student engagement. Paul combines language arts with science because "it's really much more motivating for them, it's something they're interested in instead of just learning about words and sentences." John discussed how placing too much emphasis on spelling as a separate learning area can undermine interest in writing.

> If I'm stopping them every two words and saying "How do you spell that?" then their compound, beautiful sentences might go down to only a few words, because their confidence and risk-taking will obviously be minimal at that point . . . I have a boy who came from Africa four years ago and the words he comes out with, I just don't know where he gets them from, and he understands the definitions. His spelling is horrendous . . . but his ideas are brilliant, so my argument would be, should I make his brilliance stagnate and bring him back to the spelling? I do have a spelling program, but it's not at the forefront.

Felicity was an exception in that she reported finding structured spelling lessons very motivating to her students. Perhaps the answer lies in how it is done: "word study" as distinct from "spelling" can be integrated into the program, be less threatening than spelling, and still provide some welcome routine to students.

Have special emphases in the first few weeks

Most new teachers find the early weeks of their first year very stressful (Jacklin et al., 2006). This was certainly the experience of many of our study participants. They all survived and, from what we saw, acquitted themselves well. However, the period was often quite painful, and some expressed regret at not being able to perform at a higher level: they felt badly for their students. This is in line with the comment by Bransford, Darling-Hammond, and LePage (2005) that "teachers need to serve adequately the very first students they teach" (p. 3). Whereas the principles of program planning outlined so far can certainly help during the start-up period, teachers need special ideas and strategies and a distinctive set of priorities (Fountas and Pinnell, 2001; Jacklin et al., 2006).

For example, *establishing a relatively structured program* may be necessary initially. Because so much needs to be done and everything takes longer at the beginning, new teachers may have to follow a more structured approach than they normally would. David said that a beginning teacher should "find out what program the school board mandates and . . . use it as a base, and then modify from there. Don't try to do it on your own because you'll just get overwhelmed." Liane recommended implementing "a very regular routine . . . so it can be counted on: day after day you can expect that this is what needs to be done." Vera said: "At the beginning of the year you want to do all these wonderful things, but the kids are just not ready for it." Jody postponed relatively complex group work until later in the year. "I haven't started guided reading yet [in January] . . . . You can't do everything, you have to give up something."

Conducting preliminary pupil assessment is also very important during the early period: relatively quick, informal assessment to get to know where the students are academically. Anita said a beginning teacher should "do some diagnostic assessing very early in the year . . . to find out what the students' strengths are and what they need to work on." Wanda noted that one of the skills she lacked at the beginning was "doing pre-assessments; how you go about initially assessing where your students are." Jeannie stressed the need for "a September assessment . . . trying to get them to write and see what they can do."

Building the class culture and routines should also be given special emphasis in the first few weeks, despite the pressure to begin to cover the curriculum quickly and get ready for the first report card. If the class community is well established, the time will be more than made up later in the year (Martin, 1992; Peterson, 1992). Toward the end of her third year, Sophia said:

> I spend a good two months at the beginning of the year working on rapport . . . And some people say I'm like a drill sergeant, but I'm now getting the best out of them because of it: I don't have to worry about management, all my attention is focused on the lesson and on them and what they're understanding.

Vera in March of her second year reported: "We focus at the beginning of the year on everything that is routine oriented and behavior oriented. Our first month's theme at the school is the behavior code . . . the whole school talks about behavior and what the school expects."

Many stressed the importance of *approaching others for help* during the early part of the year (Jacklin et al., 2006). Anita said a beginning teacher should "collaborate with other teachers as much as possible . . . gather as many resources as possible and sit in on a few different teachers' programs to see how they are run, to get some ideas." Felicity also spoke of seeking help, although she warned that it is not always easy: "When you're extremely overwhelmed [and] have no idea what you're doing and don't know what to ask for, that's a problem."

Finally, although the study participants gave suggestions such as these, many also said that new teachers should *just keep persevering* with their program, believing that they will steadily get on top of things and their students will learn. Tanya's advice to new teachers was to "keep trying, keep working on it . . . [The students] sometimes learn in spite of us . . . don't worry, they'll get it." Maria said:

> Be persistent, stick to it, don't give up. You'll have your days when you want to run away screaming, wondering what you got yourself into . . . and there are times when you wonder if you're good enough and you doubt yourself. But know that you are, that's why they hired you . . . And it's only your first year, don't expect to be able to do it all and be perfect. And allow yourself to make mistakes and learn from them.

Implications for pre-service education

The approach to program planning discussed in this chapter has many implications for teacher education. We note the main ones here and will deal with others in later chapters. A major underlying principle is that we cannot address all aspects of program planning in pre-service and so have to ensure that student teachers acquire an overall awareness of this dimension of teaching.

Instruction in the program planning role of the teacher

The fact that program planning is a large part of what teachers do should not come as a surprise to our graduates. While they are in the program, we need to explain more clearly the nature and importance of their planning role and give concrete examples both from experienced teachers and our own teaching. The main idea to be understood is that teachers make decisions. They do not just follow a pre-set curriculum, textbook, or program, but rather make choices about key goals and topics, classroom learning structures, materials and activities, and the sequencing, individualization, and integration of topics and activities.

As teacher educators, we need to recognize the limitations of lesson- and unit-planning assignments as a way of teaching program planning. The exercise of creating a lesson or unit for a "phantom" class tends to give student teachers an exaggerated sense of how much they will be able to cover and how much control they will have over what happens in the classroom. As we saw earlier, Candice said in her first year that having studied a "perfect program" in pre-service now "paralyzes" her. Student teachers need theory and practical advice on how to rise above the details and focus on the main things they are trying to achieve through a unit or lesson. Modeling program planning in the pre-service education program itself is a crucial means of teaching what programming is and how to do it: e.g., linking courses to one another; varying the types of teaching activities in classes; going back and forth between theory and practice; pursuing broad and important goals rather than just "covering" many disconnected topics; and modifying or entirely abandoning prepared classes as key issues arise or the mood of the students changes. As we employ these strategies and others, we should mention explicitly how they illustrate the nature and purpose of program planning.

Information and ideas about the formal "long-range plan" requirement

As noted earlier, most of the new teachers in our study had to submit a long-range plan to their principal early in the school year. We should as far as possible prepare student teachers for this task. Although the type of plan required varies, it typically consists of a timetable for dealing with strands, topics, and sub-topics within each subject over the school year, with indication of how this adheres to government and school district curricula and programs. Student teachers should be given copies of formal plans from different schools and school districts and encouraged to talk to the teachers at their practicum schools about how to approach this requirement. We need to stress that the time spent preparing a formal long-range plan should be modest, and various aids and mechanical processes should be used to get the job done as quickly as possible. We should point out that not all schools require teachers to follow their formal plan completely. And we should emphasize that a whole other planning process – also often called "long-range planning" – is needed for effective teaching. The latter is a much more important, year-long task involving constant adjustment as we gain new ideas, see what works, and get to know our students.

Information and ideas about freedom, divergence, and selectivity in teaching

Schools and school districts vary in the freedom they allow teachers. Most expect full coverage of the curriculum, but often there is latitude in the relative *emphasis* given to particular topics and in *how* the topics are taught. Student teachers should be informed about this and encouraged to find out quickly about the degree of freedom in their school. Even where there is freedom, however, a further question to be discussed in pre-service is whether and under what circumstances teachers should teach differently from their colleagues. Having a common approach has a number of advantages, but there are times when teachers should resist to some extent the programs and practices in their school.

Information and ideas about balancing structure and flexibility in programming

Student teachers are usually discouraged from adhering closely to one textbook or published program. However, too heavy an emphasis on program flexibility and "picking and choosing" materials and activities can leave new teachers with too many variables to deal with at once. Paradoxically, it can undermine their creativity as they struggle to survive. The more feasible approach we should recommend to them is not to try to improve their whole program at once but rather attend to one aspect at a time, meanwhile using at least some textbooks and programs (selectively) for guidance and support.

Theory and strategies for dealing with the ability range

One of the greatest challenges new teachers face is the range of ability in their class, and student teachers need to be informed about how wide the range is likely to be. As well as addressing this topic on the university campus, we should ensure that student teachers have opportunities to observe low-, medium-, and high-achieving pupils in their practicum classes. Further, apart from becoming aware of the ability range, student teachers need to acquire strategies for dealing with it. They should be introduced to learning materials that all pupils can appreciate and discuss together, along with open-ended learning activities that all pupils can succeed in at some level.

Practical help with organizing resources

Although having a sound conception of teaching is central to success in program planning, new teachers also need practical skills if they are to be effective planners. A key skill is being able to organize the teaching resources they collect so they can draw on them readily. In pre-service programs students teachers are given many samples of strategies and activities, but we were surprised how seldom the new teachers in our study actually used them. A strategy we have employed is to require student teachers to build a "resource kit" for the materials they gather during the program and give a brief presentation on it to a small group of peers and a faculty member once or twice during the program.

Program planning in practicum placements

In some respects, student teachers are left too much on their own in the practicum. Although the topics they teach are usually prescribed, the focus tends to be on their proving that they can single-handedly design interesting units, lessons, and activities and implement them with flare and effectiveness. A better approach often would be to have cooperating teachers show student teachers a full unit and explain how they developed it. Student teachers could then observe their cooperating teacher implementing the unit and assist with various aspects of the process. In this way they would be likely to learn much more about program planning than by simply preparing and teaching on their own.

Preparation for school start-up, especially in the first year

What to do at the beginning of the school year should be discussed as a key dimension of program planning. The special priorities at this time should be considered, including establishing structures and routines that make teaching more manageable. Student teachers should also be introduced to curriculum resources dealing with start-up. It is important not only to give generic advice but also to discuss strategies in particular subject areas, for example, types of word study or math activities that will immediately engage pupils while laying the groundwork for later approaches and learning activities.

Conclusion

Effective program planning is central to good teaching. Giving priority to instruction in program planning in pre-service education is essential if beginning teachers are to develop a sound pedagogical approach. Specific components of program planning include: (a) identifying our main teaching goals; (b) making decisions about what topics to emphasize in light of these goals; (c) balancing structure and flexibility; (d) individualizing the program; and (e) integrating the program. The first few weeks of a teacher's first year is an important time to set a pattern of selecting and prioritizing, rather than just plunging into covering a multitude of topics in preparation for the first report card.

Although much will always remain to be learned after graduation, we believe that many aspects of program planning can be introduced at the pre-service stage through theoretical and practical discussion, modeling in the campus program, and well-designed practicum experiences. Tanya's profile, presented at the beginning of the chapter, shows how working closely with able cooperating teachers in extended placements against a background of relevant theory can help a student teacher develop many of the understandings and skills of effective program planning.

Chapter 2

Pupil assessment

Pupil assessment is another high priority in teacher education. On the one hand, teachers must conduct ongoing assessment of each of their pupils in order to teach them effectively. Program planning and all other teaching activities are dependent on determining the knowledge, abilities, interests, and needs of pupils. On the other hand, and increasingly today, teachers are required to prepare their students for standardized tests, conduct some of these tests, and write complex reports for parents, government and school district officials, and others.

As with program planning, all 22 participants in our study thought their pre-service preparation in assessment was inadequate (in varying degrees). For example, in January of her first year Marisa said: "Assessment is this huge thing that is not covered enough [in pre-service] and I wish it had been." And Jeannie in March of the same year commented:

> Assessment is a big mystery right now . . . [E]veryone has their own opinion about what a Level 4 is supposed to look like, and people vary on how many A's you should give . . . . [In pre-service we needed] more on assessment.

Interestingly, the new teachers stressed this need despite the fact that the pre-service programs spent a considerable amount of time on assessment, as several of the participants acknowledged. There appears to be a mismatch here between what the pre-service faculty teach (or try to teach) and what is learned.

Over the three years of our research, however, the new teachers developed many insights into assessment. Maria's views and practices in this area seemed to us to be especially valuable.

Maria

> Now [in year 3] I have a better sense of how to do report cards. In your first year it's like, I think this kid does this; and when you go to the first parent–teacher interview, you hope the parent doesn't ask why

you assigned that grade. Now I definitely have a better picture of what the students are capable of, because I know what to expect. You can't know that until you've been teaching for a year. It's almost not fair to ask first-year teachers to give students a mark.

Background

Upon meeting Maria one is initially struck by her commanding presence, yet she is warm and friendly. Maria completed a four-year Bachelor of Arts degree in Radio and TV Broadcasting. While in the program she did an internship at a national music video TV station, but realized she was more interested in the public relations aspect than on-air work. This led her to complete a year-long postgraduate program in public relations, and on graduating she secured a full-time position in public relations; but after 9/11 the firm downsized because their work in travel and tourism declined sharply.

Maria's mother had always encouraged her to consider teaching, so with "time on her hands" she began volunteering at the elementary school she had attended as a child. Realizing that teaching was a good match with her interests and skills, she enrolled in a one-year pre-service program specializing in kindergarten to grade 6 with a focus on preparing teachers for urban schools. Over the three years since receiving her credential, Maria has been teaching grade 2 in the school she attended and where she volunteered. The neighborhood has changed dramatically since she was a student there; many of the families are struggling new immigrants living in low-rent/subsidized apartments and the school is classified as high needs.

Maria enjoyed her program in radio and TV broadcasting and believes it has helped her as a teacher because "quite obviously it's public speaking. You have to be comfortable with eye contact, talking to people, and hearing your voice. It was heavy on writing and grammar; we had a lot of English courses." She describes herself as someone who loves to read and write. Maria is also fairly positive about her pre-service program; in particular she enjoyed the literacy course, greatly admiring the instructor. She had two very successful practice teaching placements in grades 2 and 6, and her cooperating teacher from the grade 2 placement continues to be a mentor and friend. She feels that one of the limitations of teacher credential programs is that "you don't have any context, you're sitting there talking about ideal situations you haven't been in and they're not like that when you get into them. A lot of it gets washed away with reality." She would have liked very much to return to the school of education after her first year of teaching for "a summer program for people who have already taught for a year."

I now have context. I'm not just saying, If I had a student like this . . .; rather I'm saying, Look, I have this kid who came to me on the second day of school . . . Even though there was some context from the practicum, you had your mentor teacher doing all the organizing and all the day-to-day stuff.

Right from her first interview, Maria expressed strong interest in improving her assessment skills. In the first year she said: "I would love more PD on assessment. That was part of my [individual] annual plan. I want to improve on my writing program, especially, assessing writing." Maria is unusual because at an early stage in her career she has the "big picture" of assessment. She understands its connection to teaching: "It's reciprocal; we need the assessment to know what to teach." She feels that when you are planning a unit you must establish the goals for the unit and determine how it will be assessed. "It shouldn't be done at the last minute." She also feels that the students should be aware of these goals and criteria:

[W]ith my kids, I put examples of journal stories on the overhead, a level 1, 2, 3, and 4. I'll put up a level 1 and we read it and talk about it. What level is this? Why? And the kids will say: Look at all the spelling mistakes; they repeat too much; not enough detail. So we start to create our own rubrics. Look at a level 2, a level 3, 4, and make your own rubric. Then I watch what happens when they go back and write their own journal story. It's fantastic, their writing is so much better because they know what you're looking for.

In her school Maria is required to administer the DRA (developmental reading assessment); she finds it helpful for forming her guided reading groups, but sees its limitations.

I noticed a lot of kids were stuck at DRA Level 16, and I looked at that and said, You know what? I think it's the books. Look at the Level 16 book, it's about a mean man named Grumble and an elf. How much schema do my students have on elves? What do they know about that? There's no context. It's a difficult text for them.

Maria believes that she needs to work with children individually to truly determine what they have learned and ensure that no one "falls through the cracks"; for example, she uses miscue analysis, does conferencing with students individually, and designs a variety of work products for students to demonstrate what they have learned.

Learning opportunities

In analyzing our interviews with Maria, we identified five key sources of her learning about assessment.

Pre-service program

Although Maria felt insufficient time was devoted to assessment in the pre-service program, she noted some aspects that were particularly helpful. In the literacy course, she was introduced to the mandated exemplars for assessing writing; then, using samples of student writing, she worked with a group "to compare the writing and decide if this is a Level 4 or Level 2." She said this stayed with her "because we did it." The assessment strategies used by the instructors were also a good model for her.

> We used a lot of rubrics in the pre-service program, and I remember getting a project back and having the rubric all marked up. I realized the rubric told us exactly what they were looking for: you did it, and you pretty much got an A. And I realized I needed to do this with my own students.

In-school support

The grade 2 teachers in Maria's school are very strong and work as a team, holding weekly planning meetings, sharing strategies and resources, and consulting with the in-school Literacy Coordinator. Although Maria works long hours – and in her first year felt as if she was "treading water, just trying to keep afloat" – some of the burden of planning has been reduced by working closely with the team, allowing her to develop assessment methods such as a modified miscue analysis form.

Ongoing professional development

Over her first three years Maria completed a reading specialist program, and the second course in the three-part program focused on assessment. Realizing she did not know how to interpret quantitative data, she suggested to the other members of her project group that they learn how to analyze DRA scores. All agreed, and she volunteered to share the DRA scores gathered on her incoming students (the course was during the summer and the grade 1 teachers had tested each child). As a group, "we looked at all the scores, plotted them, and then looked for trends. We had different people doing different things. So I went into this year knowing where my kids were coming from, what they were capable of." She feels she now has a better understanding of ways to interpret data.

Induction program

Maria was fortunate to be in a school district that offered a good induction program. She attended in-service sessions on various topics, including assessment. She and her mentor were provided release time to use as they wished and chose to spend time learning how to write report cards. Maria felt she wanted to see practice beyond her own school, so she observed an exemplary teacher in another school, paying special attention to her assessment strategies.

Leadership activities

As noted above, Maria participated in the district-sponsored induction program. In her third year, she volunteered to help with a Summer Institute for new teachers and became heavily involved in co-planning and co-teaching the sessions. "We spent three days with all the new grade 2 teachers and I showed them my year-long plan, my daily plans, and my weekly plans. We talked them through everything." Her support continued throughout the year "and we're having a Winter Institute [next year]. They're coming [to my class] and we're going to do guided reading with them. It's an extension of what we learned in the pre-service program." It supports her view "that [first] you have to teach, then you need to come back with the context." Through her work in the Summer Institute, Maria deepened her knowledge of all aspects of curriculum and assessment and gained an interest in assuming a leadership position in the future, possibly as a curriculum consultant.

Maria's class in action

Although Maria's grade 2 classroom is very old and in desperate need of refurbishing, she has made an effort to brighten the space by displaying student work, hanging charts from clotheslines, and creating a literacy center. When the 20 students enter the room, Maria immediately calls them to the carpet to begin the math lesson. They are an extremely active group, but Maria has used a combination of well-established routines, humor, and community building to focus their energy. For example, the class have been tracking the number of steps Maria takes each day by her wearing a pedometer and charting the number daily. They have fun predicting the number of steps she has already taken that day.

The class then turn their attention to a lesson on perimeter and area, with all the children eager to participate. The lesson is highly engaging, with students using magnetic blocks to compare the difference between the perimeter and area of various two-dimensional shapes Maria has drawn on charts. The students return to their seats to complete an excellent worksheet designed by Maria. All students are on task and there is a quiet hum as they work. The students then attend a physical education class taught by a specialist teacher.

After recess, the students reconvene on the carpet for a class meeting because there has been an "incident" on the playground. Maria gently but firmly leads a discussion about community and the need for everyone to feel safe. Next, she shifts to a social studies lesson on festivals. Since it is close to Chinese New Year and many students in the class are East Asian, Maria has chosen to read a story about Imperial China. They discuss Chinese traditions, with plans to make lacey (red envelopes) for their families. They complete a worksheet on words related to Chinese New Year. Many students move seats to be with their friends, chatting as they work on their page. The day ends with them organizing their agendas and homework.

Final thoughts

Maria is a fine young teacher working in a challenging urban school; her strength in the difficult area of assessment is an indication of her talent and progress. Over her first three years she has improved in all areas of teaching, gaining confidence as her students' learning increased: her class won the Raptors Reading Program award for her school in 2007. She intends to continue her professional development, possibly enrolling in a Master of Education in the foreseeable future. Ideally, she would like to continue teaching grade 2 for at least another two more years:

> Your first year is just survival, plain and simple. In the second year you're still trying to survive but getting a little better. In third year you start getting the gears in motion, you start bringing your ideas to the table. I can see myself next year bringing more to the program, and by year five having it come to fruition.

What and why of pupil assessment

There are two main types of assessment. The first, which the new teachers often called "informal assessment," is the type most evident in Maria's case study. Following Shepard (2001), we usually refer to it as *classroom assessment* or simply *assessment* because we feel the word "informal" makes it sound sporadic and casual. In fact, this kind of assessment is (or should be) comprehensive and systematic, conducted to find out in detail what pupils know as a basis for supporting their learning. This is the only kind of assessment discussed by Cunningham and Allington in *Classrooms That Work* (2007). They say:

> Assessment is *not* grading – although assessment can help you determine and support the grades you give. Assessment is *not* standardized test scores – although these scores can give you some general idea of what children have achieved so far. Assessment *is* collecting and analyzing data to make decisions about how children are performing and growing.

(p. 160)

Similarly, Falk (2000) states that the role of what she calls "inquiry assessment" is to "look at students and their work in an open-ended way to find out what they know, how they know it, and what their strengths and vulnerabilities are" (p. 41). Genishi (1992) refers to it as "alternative assessment," saying that it is "[t]eachers' informal ways of observing and documenting development and learning" (p. 3).

The other main type of assessment is *standardized assessment*. It differs from everyday classroom assessment in that it measures a limited set of knowledge and skills thought to be of key significance. Although standardized assessment can help with teaching, it is largely done for school-wide, system-wide, and public purposes. Its standardized nature means it can be used to make comparisons from one student, class, school, school district, or government jurisdiction to another. It attempts (usually not very successfully, in our view) to indicate to the school system or the outside world the level of knowledge and skill possessed by individuals and groups, whether for research or policy purposes or as a basis for admission, graduation, employment, and so on. Falk (2000) calls this "standards-based performance assessment" (p. 59), noting that it is important for "evaluating and reporting student progress across groups" (p. 59) and as "a means to school improvement and accountability" (p. 62).

There is some overlap between everyday classroom assessment and standardized assessment. Many of our study participants said they found a degree of pedagogical value in the DRA (developmental reading assessment) and CASI (comprehension, attitudes, strategies, and interests), even though these are standardized instruments used to compare individuals and groups and give information to the outside world. Equally, those outside the classroom can benefit from the findings of everyday classroom assessment. Parents, for example, should not only receive their children's "levels" and "scores"; they should also be given specific marks in particular areas of interest and "anecdotal" information about what their children are working on, succeeding at, and struggling with. Similarly, politicians and the general public should be told about the impressive variety and depth of pupil learning taking place in classrooms.

Problems of pupil assessment

Perhaps the main problem observed among the new teachers in our study was *not understanding the nature and role of assessment*, which created difficulties for their practice. John commented:

> Coming in, I really didn't know what I should assess, what I should be looking for . . . I've kind of educated myself on it through reading and asking others. But I think it should have been covered more [in preservice] . . . how is it done, why do we do it, and what is it important to look for?

For example, because they did not understand the limitations of standardized assessment from a teaching point of view, many of the new teachers spent too much time on it, neglecting everyday classroom assessment. Also, they did not know how to relate standardized assessment to other aspects of their role such as teaching, grading, and reporting.

In addition to not understanding assessment, many of the new teachers reported *not knowing how to do it*, whether the standardized testing required by their school district or ongoing classroom assessment. Jody observed: "We talked a lot about assessment [in pre-service] but never actually had training in the two main literacy assessment tools [DRA and CASI] . . . And as far as I can see, everybody is supposed to do it, and I have been doing it." Vera noted that although assessment "was a heavy focus in the literacy program," the instructors "would tell us about a tool but not show us how to use it, or when to use it, or what kind of information it's giving you, or how it's effective." Many of the new teachers maintained that their pre-service programs should have paid greater attention to assessment that would be feasible and useful in the classroom throughout the year. Jeannie said that "informal assessment" should be addressed more fully in pre-service because formal reading inventories are "so time-consuming." In Candice's view, "working assessment was definitely a hole [in the pre-service program]."

A third problem noted by the new teachers was *not knowing how to fit assessment into their busy classroom schedule*. Some conducted very time-consuming forms of assessment in certain areas (e.g., running records, miscue analysis) and so did not have enough time left for assessment in other areas or for teaching in general. Some thought they *should* be doing more assessment of certain types and became anxious when they did not have the time for it. Anita in her second year said she had not had time to do systematic note-taking on her students and she felt badly about this; she planned to try to do more in the future and "see if I can keep it up." Maria, though very conscientious in assessment as we have seen, reported feeling that she should be doing more: "There are so many other ways out there."

A fourth set of problems had to do with *the challenges of marking and reporting*. These were of many kinds:

- Too time-consuming

  Felicity: "Marking language assignments [has been difficult]. I think we did quite well [in pre-service] in terms of learning about rubrics and things . . . But I'm stuck with piles and piles of creative writing that I asked the kids to generate and I just have no idea how to find time to mark them. So I think I could have had more instruction on that."

- Disparity between the current government assessment system and parents' understanding of grades

Anita: "I find there's a discrepancy between letter grades and levels. A lot of my kids get very discouraged if they're getting B's and their parents say they have to bring home A's . . . Parents are used to A's being good or being the best, but in the government curriculum B is at grade level and is actually very good."

• Parents not finding the report cards useful, intelligible

Wanda: "I think quite honestly that the report card for primary does a disservice to the child and to the parents: it doesn't really tell the parents how their child is doing . . . We have to put in canned comments that are all very similar . . . we don't have the space or opportunity to really tell about the child."

• Discouraging students

Paul: "There are some students who I think need more marks to motivate them, but when I give them more marks and actually tell them what they got they get discouraged, feeling: 'I put my heart and soul into that and you didn't give me an A, so what's the point of really trying hard on the next one?'." Anita: "[Assessment] is still [in year 3] one of the most difficult things I have to do; when I have a stack of papers to mark, I cringe at having to actually give a student a grade or a level. It's the least enjoyable part of my job."

A fifth problem with assessment – one the new teachers appeared to have only moderate awareness of – is that *it can actually do a considerable amount of harm*. All types of assessment can go wrong if not used appropriately. Even everyday classroom assessment can be harmful if it leads to excessive emphasis on "skills and drills" and rote learning of facts – e.g., word spellings, grammar rules, science formulas, historical dates – to the neglect of understanding and more important skills. With respect to standardized assessment, its common harmful effects have been well documented in the research literature (e.g., Cunningham and Allington, 2007; Darling-Hammond, Ancess, and Falk, 1995; Falk, 2000; Shepard, 1991; Shepard, 2001; Shepard, Hammerness, Darling-Hammond, and Rust, 2005; Sleeter, 2005). These include: (i) narrowing the goals of teaching to a sub-set, many of which are relatively trivial in nature; (ii) fostering in students an excessive preoccupation with fragmented information, test scores, and career advancement; (iii) stereotyping, ability grouping, tracking, and grade-retention of pupils in ways that harm their self-image, reduce their learning, and disadvantage them academically and occupationally; and (iv) simply wasting time through excessive teaching-to-the-test and coaching in test-taking skills, not to mention the time involved in the testing itself.

Principles and strategies of pupil assessment

We now present some of the principles and strategies of pupil assessment we think should be discussed with student teachers if they are to understand the area and develop the skills they need. These are just a beginning, since many issues in the area are still unclear and student teachers themselves will have much to contribute. In developing these ideas we have again drawn on both the literature in the field and our longitudinal study of the experiences and views of new teachers.

Connect assessment to teaching

We believe that the key step in developing a sound approach to assessment is to link it closely to teaching (as illustrated in Maria's profile). Problems arise when assessment is seen mainly as a "foreign" task performed for purposes other than teaching. The goals and scope of our assessment should, as far as the system allows, be the same as for our instructional program in the classroom. Many of the new teachers in our study struggled initially with assessment, and this was partly because they saw it as separate from teaching. When confronted with the enormous demands of their teaching role, especially in the first year, they wondered how they could find room for assessment and why it was necessary to do so.

Many of these new teachers, however, soon saw the importance of assessment for teaching, and they overcame the problem of shortage of time by integrating assessment more into their teaching activities. For example, Nancy reported:

> First of all, I have my students do something that's in my literacy program – a little assignment, a writing piece – to see where they are. And if I see they have a problem with tenses or use too much slang or whatever, I'll go and cover those things.

And Carrie, teaching a grade 8 special needs class, said she did an initial assessment that showed her that her students were "about at a grade 6 level, so my goals should be lowered and reasonable . . . So the data really have driven the specific things we are working on."

The degree of emphasis on connecting assessment to teaching appeared to increase over the period of the study. For example, in March of her second year Felicity described how her understandings and practices regarding assessment had changed: "You start to calm down a bit . . . in the second year, you start to be able to observe the students better." With this outlook, she found she could incorporate assessment more easily into her daily activities as a teacher:

> As you teach more, you start to make more visceral – for want of a better word – assessments. You know where your children are and what they're capable of . . . [E]very day, you're doing little mini-assessments on the students and saying "Well, their writing has improved" or "This is the area they're having difficulty with." So I find I'm a lot more practical in how I'm using assessments; because it's "Oh this is what's happening, well let's address that," rather than pen-and-paper and marking assignments type assessment.

Vera, who had wondered about the place of assessment in her first year, stated emphatically in March of her second year: "I think the assessment piece is really, really key: knowing how to get at the students' learning and how to take the next step." By the end of her third year, she felt she had made yet more progress in this area:

> I've gotten a lot better at tracking student progress and using that information to inform the teaching I do with my kids. I'm better at diagnosing a group of kids in reading, for example, seeing that they're weak at returning to a word they've skipped, and then teaching that to them again. Or I'll see that my whole class has no idea what re-telling is, so we'll have a whole unit on re-telling and do it to death . . . Because there's no point moving on if they don't have that foundation.

In several cases, the link between assessment and teaching was institutionalized at the school level, and the new teachers saw the value in this. In her second year, Anita noted that the junior (grades 4–6) teachers at her school meet as grade teams and decide what they want their students to learn.

> We talk about evaluation and do the CASI tests all together . . . and do a visual representation of where the students are and their needs, which has been really helpful. So this year my program is more focused in terms of, for instance, I need to teach my students about conventions, finding the main idea, summarizing, and reading skills. So that has been my focus for whatever I build into the classroom.

Later in the same year she said this collaborative assessment program "gives us as teachers a focus for the next term or the next year . . . It drives the programming." Marisa described a similar group effort at her school:

> As a whole school . . . we're going to use First Steps to assess the students, decide what part of the developmental continuum they're on in their writing, and then use this as a way of programming . . . eventually developing a school plan for writing – which grades will cover which

conventions or writing forms – so there is more consistency, rather than overlaps or gaps.

Limit the emphasis on standardized assessment

The other side of the coin of connecting classroom assessment to teaching is putting standardized assessment in perspective. It is crucial to recognize that standardized testing assesses only a sub-set of learnings and so is of limited significance from a teaching point of view. It measures only a small part of what pupils need to know, and what teachers need to know in order to support pupil learning (Darling-Hammond, Ancess, and Falk, 1995; Falk, 2000). Accordingly, teachers should not give standardized assessment too large a place in their planning and teaching. Some special preparation should be given in relevant content and test-taking skills, because of what is at stake. But the main focus should be on fostering deep, important learning (Otero, 2006).

Initially, many of the new teachers in our study appeared to us to place too much emphasis on formal reading assessments, especially DRA or CASI. They were very concerned if they did not have time to administer these tests and tended to give them priority over other forms of assessment. However, some saw their limits rather quickly. For example, Marisa in her first year commented:

> I do the DRA . . . but also I try as much as possible to . . . just listen to the students reading, making sure they're reading something above their level . . . [To a beginning teacher I would say] be on top of the students and keep pulling them aside for five minutes and listening to them read, because even that five minutes will give you so much information about what stage they're at and how they're doing.

John in both the first and second year said that, although he regards the DRA as important, he uses other methods as well and thinks "anecdotals are huge." He stressed the need to take more account of reading comprehension than the DRA does.

> Is [what we're assessing] just decoding words? No it's not, it's reading comprehension . . . I've got a boy in my class who can read a Level 44 text really well, but when you ask him what the book is about he can't tell you very much.

Once again, we noticed progress over the time of the study in the participants' awareness of the limits – and in some case the harmfulness – of standardized assessment. In her second year, Vera commented that she was now placing less emphasis on the DRA.

> One thing I [did differently this year] was . . . not just using DRA
> but using other things like their concept of print and how they see
> themselves as readers . . . I'm still not totally sure how to use DRA
> effectively, but at least I see now that it's just one of many assessment
> tools you can use to see how to get at their learning.

Also in her second year, Sophia said that she uses CASI for certain purposes
in her teaching but then added: "Could I still run a good literacy program
without CASI? Yes, I think I could." Turning from reading inventories to
the government's large-scale literacy and math testing program (EQAO),
some of the new teachers by their third year had become quite vocal in
their concerns. Tanya, whose class was in a testing year (grade 3), commented:

> I was infuriated during EQAO testing this year, I had an awful three
> days. And our VP knew how hard I was struggling and said to me:
> "It's okay, it'll be fine, it'll be over in three days and you can go back
> to whatever you wanted to do." He was quite supportive, but it was
> hard because I felt that what I was putting the students through was
> so wrong.

Along the same lines, David said:

> Public education is not headed in the direction I think it should be.
> Standardized testing – EQAO especially – drives everything we do;
> we see it, we hear it in in-service, it's just a huge push. And I'm think-
> ing to myself, that represents what a kid did one day for three hours,
> it doesn't reflect who that child is. And just because a child scores a
> level 2, that doesn't mean they're not going to be Prime Minister of
> this country . . . Our former Minister of Education was a high school
> drop-out. So to push these standards is to marginalize kids who can't
> perform on a paper and pencil test. And that's ironic, because when
> you go to teachers' college, the first thing they tell you is that assess-
> ment is not about paper and pencil tests.

Use many kinds of assessment

Once teachers come to see assessment as primarily to gain information for
teaching, they realize it should ideally be as comprehensive and individualized as teaching itself. Accordingly, many different kinds of assessment are
needed. As Sophia noted in her third year:

> My philosophy of assessment is holistic: there's not one method that's
> more important than another. There's oral assessment when we're in
> a large group . . . small-group assessment when, for example, kids are

doing experiments together or collaborating on a problem . . . [and] there are culminating activities . . . . To me, every assessment is attached to a different kind and level of understanding . . . . You end up getting a better sense of a child when there are a bunch of different ways.

Paul, working in a special needs class in his third year, said:

> Because they're doing individual work, [the assessment tools] are totally different for each student . . . [I]n science, math, and social studies assessment is more based on drawing, talking, and so on than in the past . . . Because some of them are very smart and they've learned a lot by following the units and participating, but they can't write it down.

We note below several of the assessment methods used by the new teachers, along with brief quotations that indicate reasons for using them and how they go about it.

- Observation in the whole class

  Wanda: "I run very few true sit-down tests. Part of the reason is that my children have real difficulty sitting and doing their own work. So a lot of my assessment comes from observation, discussion, work in class."

  Sophia: "I see their participation each day, their experiment worksheets, how they work in their experiment groups, who participates on the carpet, who's thinking outside the box and asking interesting questions."

- Observation in small groups (guided reading groups, collaborative groups, centers, etc.)

  Anita: "As they do [guided reading with me] I get to see how they're thinking, the kinds of things they're thinking about . . . ways I can help them improve . . . whether they are paying attention to punctuation when they read, using it to help them understand the text, sounding out the words, making inferences, and so on; and I watch for what's lacking, and either right then or next week, we'll talk about a particular skill or a bunch of things."

- Observation in one-on-one settings

  Wanda: "I do some diagnostic assessment . . . but it's much more observation and talking and just one-on-one conferences, sitting down with them and actually seeing what they can do."

- Self- and peer-assessment

  Sophia: "In literacy, I expect groups to assess themselves, and individual students to assess themselves, before I do my own assessing. I want to hear what they have to say; and I find they're often pretty much right on, like just a minus or a plus from what I would give them."

- Tests and assignments on specific topics

  David (teaching grade 7): "I tried some fairly substantial summative assignments and it was too much for them; it overwhelmed them . . . So I do a lot more formative assessment now, and when I do do a summative, it's very specific, targeted on maybe one or two expectations that we've been hitting on frequently over the course of maybe three weeks."

- Open-ended assignments

  Sophia: "I don't like assessing through tests; rather, I do culminating tasks with lots of hands-on experiences . . . Like just recently we were studying rocks and minerals, and the culminating task was to create a rock poster. Instead of a test, I give them something fun to express themselves."

- Modified standardized testing

  Sophia: "I used CASI once diagnostically . . . But what I did was . . . let them pick something that was relevant."

  Marisa: "At end of first term I assessed them . . . on parts of CASI, just the ones I taught . . . to see if they had learned what I had taught."

- Oral assessment

  Maria: "I don't think it's fair to base their reading mark on a written response, because there are students who can't express themselves very well in writing but can retell the story orally, and why shouldn't that count? So we need to assess in different ways."

- Written assessment

  Nina: "Because my class is fairly small, with 19 students, I have an intuitive sense of each child; but you absolutely have to have something in your hand."

• Collection and examination of rough work and polished work

Nina: "I have each student's writing journal, which is all their rough copies; and their portfolio, which is either peer-edited or edited with help from me."

Develop a feasible program of assessment

One of the main problems we saw in our study was that new teachers tried (or hoped) to carry out types of assessment that were not really possible in the time available. This led to their feeling inadequate and frustrated; or where they did do what they intended, they were left without time for other more important teaching activities and forms of assessment. It is essential that new teachers develop an approach to assessment that is feasible for them and optimally supports their teaching program.

Part of the secret here is to limit the emphasis on standardized testing (including literacy inventories). As discussed earlier, such assessment takes up a lot of time and covers only a small proportion of what we need to find out. But even everyday classroom assessment can be overly time-consuming if it is too formal, resulting in neglect of other key activities. For example, teachers should weigh how much time they can afford to spend on methods such as running records, miscue analysis, and other kinds of systematic note taking. To the extent that written records are necessary, recording tools such as checklists should be developed or borrowed that take up as little time as possible. Wanda in her third year spoke about her relatively informal approach to assessment:

[In terms of useful, reliable assessment] I do a lot of observation . . . I do a minimal amount of testing, because some kids don't do well in a formal assessment situation. I assess mainly through observing, conversing, taking a look at their day-to-day materials . . . I have them do little projects [which I assess], but it's largely just their regular work that shows me where they are.

In our view, although making notes on individual students has a place, we should not be so preoccupied with it that we fail to get to know our students in a more comprehensive way. In this regard, the case of Maria (profiled earlier) is instructive. As we saw, she is a talented, hardworking teacher who has been very successful in assessing, program planning, and community building. Yet she felt she should be doing more assessment: "There are so many other ways out there"; in particular, she wants to do more "research" in her classroom. However, we believe she should be careful. She might embark on forms of documentation that are too time-consuming, resulting in her not being able to maintain the kind of responsive, vibrant classroom culture she has at present. She may also lose some of the enjoyment of work in the classroom, of which she spoke often. Perhaps she should try to add just one new assessment method at a time and see how it goes, a gradualist approach to program development often recommended (e.g., Hubbard and Power, 1993).

On the whole, the study participants became better at quick and informal (yet comprehensive) kinds of assessment over the period of the study. In interviews toward the end of the third year, Paul said:

> Just from working with them, teachers know their students and what levels they're at, and as long as they're communicating that to the students, I'm not sure you have to make rubrics for everything and do the kinds of things that sound good in a workshop but that you really don't have time for.

Vera commented:

> I don't DRA the kids all the time and I don't take a lot of running records, which I know I should [laughing]. But [I find it's often enough] just to listen to the kids or see – either in a small group or one-on-one – where their errors are and what they still need to work on.

Anita noted:

> I've been doing a lot more conferencing with my students, especially for literacy, one on one. As they're working I go around and jot down little notes about how they're doing, or I ask them "Well, what are you doing today as a writer (or reader)?" and they tell me and I jot down where they are so that I can guide them better . . . [Or] I make checklists for writing assignments – what's been taught and what's expected – and then check off what they've accomplished.

Individualize assessment

Just as teaching must be individualized, as discussed in Chapter 1, so must assessment. To be able to address the learning needs of individual students we have to find out as far as possible their *distinctive* abilities and challenges (Jablon, Dombro, and Dichtelmiller, 1999). This is also necessary if we are to give students due credit for their talents and achievements (Sleeter, 2005). For example, a student who is weak in formal writing may be strong in dealing with complex social situations, such as those found in the workplace or the community. Although formal writing is important, it is not the only type of skill that should be acknowledged and rewarded (Meier, 1995).

The new teachers we studied saw the necessity of finding out about the individual interests and attainments of students and taking these into account in teaching. Candice commented that "students should be working at their own level, should be encouraged from where they are." Vera said that some of her students "couldn't decode that well but they had really good storytelling skills and comprehension skills." And Sophia noted the importance of assessing oral ability: "Sometimes I sit them down to write a test and they can't do it, whereas if I have a conversation with them it's amazing what will come out of their mouth."

A specific need for individualized assessment mentioned by some of the new teachers was in the area of learning styles. This is a matter not so much of distinctive challenges and attainments as of how students learn most effectively, and it has implications for *how* we teach them. Maria reported:

> I have my students read silently for 20 minutes a day . . . and while they're reading, I take a different child each day and have them read whatever book they're on . . . [and] I can tell who's reading for meaning, who's a visual learner, whether they say 'Chris' instead of 'Christmas,' 'wishes' instead of 'wish,' and so on . . . And I'm learning . . . how to analyze that information to inform my teaching.

Wanda said:

> I did a survey of learning styles with this Grade 3 class and it was eye-opening to find out that the students I thought would be kinesthetic in their style of learning tended to be more auditory. So I'm going to try to do that and also going to ask for parental input in terms of how they see their child's learning style.

A more controversial aspect of individualized assessment is assigning different students the same mark or level when their knowledge and skills are different. Sophia spoke of the need to give two students the same letter grade when in fact one may be strong in writing and the other in oral skills. Wanda emphasized that different students must often be given the same grade or level designation for different attainments: "Given the differences, it's hard to mark one student versus another because within each individual student there are successes, whether or not they have been able to achieve certain benchmark levels with reading assessments or writing conventions."

Wanda had a particular concern about how the use of rubrics can lead to stereotyping of students. Although she uses them, she recognizes that having the same guidelines for all students may standardize their approach to a task and also our assessment of their performance. Tanya contrasted her guided reading program, which utilizes government and school district rubrics on fluency and comprehension levels, with her literacy circle discussions "which I'm loving because it's a different form of comprehension."

Another difficult area in the individualization of assessment is the practice of giving higher grades to IEP (individual education plan) and ELL students than they would normally receive for the equivalent performance. Nina said she was "not comfortable" with this approach because

> a lot of times I'm talking to parents through interpreters, and they see their child is getting Bs and Cs and they're thinking "Oh, everything is cool," whereas their child is actually functioning a grade below; and they don't seem to get that. So I think the report card is a little misleading.

Although this practice serves important purposes – giving encouragement to low-performing students, allowing them to participate with their peers, and enabling them to go on to the next grade – care must be taken to ensure that students, parents, and teachers at the next grade level understand the accommodations that have been made and the reasons for them.

Assess authentically

If it is to be useful, assessment must be authentic, that is, "real" or "genuine." It must (a) *actually assess* what it sets out to assess, and (b) assess what is *important* from an educational and, ultimately, real-life point of view. The need for authentic assessment in this twofold sense is emphasized by Darling-Hammond, Ancess, and Falk (1995), who recommend that teachers assess by means of projects, portfolios, oral presentations, and "performance-oriented tasks . . . rather than focusing merely on recall and recognition of facts . . . Rather than administering standardized multiple choice tests that are several steps removed from actual literacy activities," teachers should "watch their students at work" (pp. 1–2). And "rather than assembling disconnected pieces of information," the assessment tasks should be "set in a meaningful context" that connects to "real-world experiences" (p. 4).

The new teachers in our study were in certain ways clearly attuned to authentic assessment as outlined above. This is apparent from the features of their assessment described earlier. Connecting assessment to teaching, limiting emphasis on standardized tests, using many kinds of assessment, and individualizing assessment all help ensure that teachers' assessment is focused on what they are actually trying to measure and teach rather than incomplete or superficial markers of learning.

However, many of our study participants did not seem sufficiently aware of the need to connect school learning – no matter how well taught and validly assessed – to real-world purposes. We found considerable preoccupation with teaching and assessment of government and school district "expectations" that are often rather standardized and removed from everyday life. Of course, there is a limit to the extent to which teachers – especially new teachers – can depart from the broad outlines of officially mandated school learning. However, as discussed in the previous chapter, teachers often have more freedom than they think to decide which topics to emphasize and how much to relate them to the real world.

Marking and reporting: apply the same assessment principles

Marking tests and assignments for reporting purposes is a somewhat distinctive activity. It tends to be "summative," that is, *final* assessment rather than aimed at promoting learning, and is addressed in part to an outside audience (mainly parents). However, in line with the first general principle of assessment discussed earlier, teachers should as far as possible *connect marking and reporting to the teaching program* as well. Along these lines, Carrie said:

> I mark their reading response journals every week, so by the end of the term I have 12 marks from that [for the report cards], which is good because you can see a trend, whether they are improving or not . . . And I respond to the students . . . and pose questions to them, and sometimes put in something else like "I'd like to see more detail" or "I'm glad to see you're using paragraphs here."

Similarly, Felicity described how her approach to marking is in keeping with her teaching objectives.

> When I was younger in school, it was all about grammar and spelling. But from my teacher training program and being in the classroom, [I now think] we should focus on what we want to teach. So with the students' journal entries, I no longer cover them with red pen marks because what I'm looking for is that the students can express a concept or an idea or a feeling, and add detail into their writing.

Another general principle of assessment that applies to marking and reporting is that of *using many measures*. The new teachers felt marks should be assigned on the basis of a variety of considerations, such as comprehension, writing skill, oral ability, work completion, and so on. For example, Marisa said:

> I'm trying not to rely too much on written responses as I find it doesn't always give me the best sense of what they know, because some of them – especially the boys – just write down as much as they need to finish

and hand it in, not really showing you what they know. So writing isn't the best way to assess their reading, it's more their oral response, listening to their discussions and the questions they ask.

Assessing *authentically* is another general principle relevant to marking and reporting. Some of the new teachers stressed the need to dig below the surface and capture what is really important for learning and for life beyond the school. For example, Carrie spoke of how she refuses to give high marks to students just because they complete everything and are "perfect on the test." Similarly, as we have seen, Felicity focuses her marking largely on whether her students can express concepts, ideas, and feelings rather than on conventions such as spelling and grammar. Wanda spoke of needing to be more genuinely informative in reporting to parents, indicating that "these are the strengths, these are the areas of concern, this is what we need to work on, and this is how your kid's doing."

Finally, as with assessment generally, marking and reporting activities should be *feasible*. They should not take up so much time that teachers become exhausted or are forced to neglect other aspects of their role. David talked about having to maintain a balance between too little and too much marking, given "the regular first-year teaching load." Nina, while acknowledging the need to have something concrete to show to parents, said she really only marks the students' writing journal, because that is the main thing they do themselves. Anita described how she saves time by combining finding out about students for teaching purposes with getting ready to complete the required reports:

> I'm finding I'm much less stressed this year [year 2] doing report cards, because I'm circulating around my class all the time and always reading their writing and getting them to read to me and so on, so I have a better sense of where they're at, even if I haven't written it down. So I feel more confident that I'm giving them an appropriate mark this year than I was last year.

Implications for pre-service education

Pupil assessment is difficult for new teachers to master prior to full-time experience with a class of their own across a school year. However, we believe a better job could be done in this area in pre-service by explaining more clearly the basic nature and purpose of assessment. Many of the problems of our study participants arose from attaching too much significance to formal assessment and not enough to everyday classroom assessment, which is in fact much more important. In addition, they often lacked practical strategies in classroom assessment.

Clearer understanding of the relationship between assessment and teaching

At present in pre-service education we often portray assessment as a rather technical task carried out for external purposes such as reporting to parents, government agencies, and higher education institutions. Because the technical aspects are difficult, we tend to spend a lot of time on them and as a result neglect everyday classroom assessment. Alternatively, because we view formal assessment as technical we sometimes bring in specialists to teach about it. This again can mean that everyday assessment for teaching does not receive enough attention.

In our view we should strongly reject this approach, emphasizing from the beginning that assessment is mainly a classroom-based activity aimed at supporting teaching. The program-planning and decision-making role of the teacher should be stressed, and assessment then explained in this context: it provides comprehensive knowledge of our students so we can make better programming decisions. To the extent that we arrange separate instruction on assessment in pre-service, we should ensure that it reinforces the connection to teaching. To a large degree, pre-service instruction in assessment should be conducted within C&I (curriculum and instruction) courses, thus enabling us to give subject-based examples of how assessment serves teaching.

Clearer understanding of the limited value of standardized assessment

Linking assessment to teaching goes hand in hand with explaining the limited usefulness of standardized assessment. As we saw earlier, new teachers typically come away from pre-service believing that standardized assessment (including DRA, CASI, and other formal inventories) is the main form of assessment, and this has a distorting effect on their assessment and teaching practices. Our suggestion is that standardized assessment should receive much less air time in pre-service, and when we do discuss it, we should emphasize that (a) it measures only a narrow band of student abilities and attainments, and (b) it often does a great deal of harm, causing students considerable distress, undermining their self-esteem, misrepresenting their knowledge and abilities, and diverting teachers from more important forms of teaching, learning, and assessment.

Greater familiarity with everyday assessment methods in feasible forms

To illustrate the relationship between assessment and teaching and provide student teachers with the repertoire of classroom assessment methods they need, we should devote considerable time in pre-service to the theory and practice of everyday assessment methods. In doing so, we should ensure that the methods studied are feasible in the overall life and work of the classroom. From what we have seen, many of the classroom assessment methods recommended in texts and taught in pre-service – e.g., running records, miscue analysis, formal individual interviews – are too time-consuming for actual implementation, unless they are modified to a substantial degree. As our study participants pointed out, much quicker methods – in some cases not involving record keeping at all – are needed if they are to be able to get to know all their students in the comprehensive manner required for teaching.

Clearer understanding of the need to get to know each child individually

Many new teachers leave pre-service with insufficient awareness of how different pupils attain the "same" level in different ways, and why such diversity is essential for optimal learning and development. They tend to assume that all pupils should acquire the same knowledge and skills, although in different degrees because of different levels of talent and motivation. This outlook prevents them from seeing the complexity of assessment, the importance of getting to know each child individually, and the need to engage in assessment almost every moment of the school day.

The concept of multiple intelligences is now almost universally taught in pre-service programs. In our view, this concept leads logically and importantly to a notion of individualized assessment that should also receive substantial attention in pre-service. In writing, for example, two students should both be able to attain a "high" level even though one excels in vivid, imaginative expression and the other in tight, persuasive argument. If we wish to indicate the difference between the two in a report, we must use anecdotal comments, portfolio selections, or the like. We cannot give one a higher writing grade than the other and remain consistent with the multiple intelligences position.

Help with the theory and practice of marking and reporting

Student teachers need more instruction in how to negotiate marking and reporting requirements. Fulfilling these requirements can easily take up so much time that it undermines essential teaching activities. All the participants in our study reported major difficulties in this area, especially in their first year. Practical advice is required, along with discussion of fundamental issues such as what constitutes useful, "authentic" marking, how much time should be spent on marking, and how is it possible to fulfill our institutional reporting obligations while offering parents and students genuinely informative feedback.

Conclusion

There are two main types of assessment: standardized assessment and everyday classroom assessment. The latter type (sometimes called "informal assessment") is much more important than the former but unfortunately often receives less attention in pre-service education and writings on assessment. Classroom assessment enables us to get to know pupils' knowledge, needs, and interests in the comprehensive and individualized manner necessary to support their learning. In order to do it successfully, we need to understand the close connection between assessment and teaching, and also have a large repertoire of assessment methods that can feasibly be integrated into our teaching program and the life of the classroom.

In pre-service preparation we should give high priority to instruction in pupil assessment. In doing so, however, most attention should be devoted to the theory and practice of everyday classroom assessment. To the extent that we address standardized assessment, our main focus should be on explaining its narrow scope and other limitations; the harm that it frequently does; the political forces at work in the design and imposition of standardized assessment programs; and how to negotiate system requirements for standardized assessment in a way that minimizes the harm and leaves room for a sound teaching program and comprehensive classroom assessment.

Chapter 3

Classroom organization and community

The priorities for teacher education we have discussed so far are program planning and pupil assessment. A third area needing emphasis is the *setting* in which teaching and learning takes place: the structures, routines, social patterns, and atmosphere of the classroom. The classroom environment must be one that supports student learning (including personal growth generally), rather than undermining it. Students have difficulty learning if, for example, they are constantly interrupted, are unclear what to do next, feel unsafe or insecure, or have little connection with the teacher or their peers.

The new teachers in our study quickly saw the importance of the classroom setting but often had difficulty dealing with it, even where it had received considerable attention in their pre-service program. Small-group work and behavior management they found particularly challenging. Once again we see an intriguing mismatch between what the pre-service faculty thought they were teaching and what the new teachers felt they learned in pre-service. In this chapter we make some suggestions regarding this area, based on the new teachers' experiences and views and the literature in the field. We begin with a profile of Anita, a study participant who seemed especially adept at organizing her classroom and creating a positive atmosphere.

Anita

> Part of building community is me treating students with respect, talking to them respectfully, and not being condescending. When the students feel they are valued, respected, and listened to, then they feel safe and secure. They feel they can do their best work and they pass that respect on to others and to the teacher.

Background

Anita, a gentle, thoughtful teacher in her late twenties, completed a one-year postbaccalaureate pre-service program at OISE/UT with a specialization in teaching history (or social studies), giving her the credential to teach grades 4 through 10. In her initial three years of teaching she worked in two markedly different schools, teaching a grade 5 class half-time in literacy and math the first year and a combined grade 4/5 class the next two years with responsibility for most curriculum subjects. In the first year she was not able to secure a permanent position until October, when she was hired to teach mornings only a newly-formed grade 5 class with students drawn from the other grade 5 classes in the school. This urban school had a high proportion of minority students, mainly of Middle-Eastern, South Asian, and South-East Asian heritage, most from a low socioeconomic background. Her first year of teaching was extremely challenging because her students understandably resented being uprooted from their original classes in mid-semester, and many were performing well below grade level; but in spite of the situation, she successfully built community. She felt supported by the principal and other teachers and worked much longer hours than her half-time appointment required.

Anita's undergraduate degree included a double major in psychology and linguistics, which she felt was a useful background for teaching. Her pre-service program was cohort-based and framed by a social constructivist philosophy, with the principles of inquiry, integration, and community shaping the curriculum and the entire experience. The faculty in the program spent substantial time building community through a range of activities: a two-day retreat at the beginning of the year, cohort socials for students and faculty throughout the year, explicit discussion of community and learning, and modeling of collaborative learning techniques such as literature circles. She noted that the program had a strong influence on her goals and practices as a teacher.

> I came away from pre-service with this feeling that I wanted to build a positive community in my class, and that has been an explicit goal on my part. I didn't really have that as a goal going into the program, so I think it affected me that way . . . drawing my attention to how important community is.

The importance of community and the need for effective classroom management strategies were reinforced in Anita's practice teaching placements. One of her mentor teachers excelled in building community:

> Marg was very into treating students with respect and making sure everyone felt comfortable. I learned that you have to have a strong community before any sort of deep learning can take place . . . How Marg spoke to the students and how she dealt with the students showed that she had a great deal of respect for the students and they could tell that. She had an amazing manner about her, very approachable, very respectful.

Anita felt she learned a great deal about classroom management from her instructors in the academic program, many of whom were experienced teachers; they spent considerable time addressing goals and strategies relevant to this area. Also she participated in Tribes training (Gibbs, 2000) during the program which helped her learn additional principles and strategies.

Description of practice

We found Anita to be exceptionally able in classroom management and community building. Her classroom has a calm atmosphere; students work well together; there is a spirit of support and collaboration; routines are firmly established; student misbehavior is dealt with swiftly and in a positive way. Anita knows her students well; students are responsible for maintaining a supportive culture; very difficult students are repeatedly given inviting messages to join the community; and humor is used to diffuse tense situations and create a unique class culture. Anita believes it is "the teacher's responsibility to keep the kids engaged. I don't think we should put the onus on the kids . . . It's our job to facilitate their engagement, how they're interacting with each other and approaching their work."

Anita's skills evolved over the three years. She came to see more clearly that community does not just "happen"; she purposefully engages in community-building activities, employing many of the strategies that were used in her pre-service cohort. At the heart of her philosophy is the belief that it is essential to know her students as individuals, becoming aware of topics that interest them or challenges in their home situation. We can see the influence on her of the social constructivist philosophy of her teacher education program. She recalled learning in the program "the theory of how to facilitate kids talking about books and figuring out the parts they enjoyed and making the experience enjoyable for them . . . If it doesn't have meaning for them, they're not going to be engaged and excited by reading and writing."

Anita recognizes that community building is not restricted to formal Tribes activities or other special techniques; it also has to be part of her regular academic program. For example, she employs a range of class groupings: whole class, self-selected groups, ability groups, teacher-selected groups, randomly created groups, and individual work. Throughout the day, students have many opportunities to interact with each other. She reconstitutes the groups regularly to prevent ability grouping from harming student self-esteem.

Group work can be challenging for beginning teachers. Around the middle of her first year of teaching Anita formed guided reading groups, but she found the management of them somewhat problematic. The principal, a very effective curriculum leader, offered suggestions for program planning and also arranged for Anita to observe experienced teachers managing group work. Through these observation sessions Anita came to realize that changes in her practices were needed, although she was reassured to find that classroom management is an ongoing concern for all teachers. She became stronger in establishing routines and effective group activities and making her literacy program more engaging for her students.

By the third year, Anita's skills in classroom management were exemplary. Of special note is the way she makes expectations for student work and behavior transparent, in part by involving students in setting expectations. The following is an example she gave of how she realizes this goal.

> In first term, the students learned many writing skills, and for their final project they needed to use all these skills. Before they wrote the project I said, "Based on what we've been learning, what do you think I'm going to assess you on?" They gave me a list of all the things that we had been doing in class. I added one or two points and then I said, "Okay, this is a checklist of how I'm going to mark you." We also talked about what levels 1, 2, 3, and 4 [on the rubric] might include. I find creating rubrics with the kids helps a lot.

Anita's class in action

At the end of her second year Anita was declared "surplus" at her original school, but luckily she secured a position in a neighboring school, also in the core of the city but in an area undergoing gentrification. The students come from both affluent and less well-off families. The staff are welcoming, helpful, and cohesive, with a principal who has a very democratic approach to decision making. Anita sees the staff as a community and feels there is a collective sense of responsibility for the children's learning and well-being.

Anita's classroom is bright and cheerful with student work in art and core subjects on display. Motivational posters line the walls and charts with helpful hints for working with others are hung across the room. On a day when we visited her, students eagerly entered the classroom and were warmly greeted by Anita who asked specific questions or made encouraging comments, clearly revealing her knowledge of each child. It is a combined grade 4/5 class yet the students mingle easily with each other. The day began with an imaginative word-study exercise in which each student gave a presentation on 10 words they had selected during their independent reading that they found interesting or believed could help them with their writing. As the students shared their words the rest of the class listened closely, and all were comfortable asking or responding to questions. Some students presented on quite advanced vocabulary whereas others had chosen simpler words, yet there was general support for all. When one student made an inappropriate comment, Anita reminded him about the type of talk allowed in their community. It was a firm but not aggressive response.

The students then moved to the bank of computers in the library to work on their social studies projects. They were using the computer program *Smart Ideas* to generate a web of ideas on a social studies topic, followed by a final report. Although these were individual projects – on citizenship and the rights and responsibilities of governments – the children helped each other. For example, one student was not sure where to put agriculture on her web because, as she said, "it is not really a natural resource." As students made suggestions it was apparent they had learned skills and attitudes for giving feedback and assisting each other. All were on task, but they also conversed easily about personal interests (Are you going to try out for the swim team?) and the social studies project (How many ideas do you have in your web?).

During recess, Anita worked with students in the folk dancing club she organized. There was a strong sense of camaraderie among the students and between her and the students as they practiced their dances. After recess, Anita gave a presentation to the whole class on the mathematics of making change. She then divided them into heterogeneous groups she had pre-selected to work on making change for various "purchases" from the class store. She made clear beforehand the expectations, for example that each student must have a turn and group members are responsible for helping each other. When the class became too noisy, she used a rain stick to get their attention. At the end of the group work, Anita had the whole class reconvene to debrief on the process of the group work and their learning, which they did honestly, respectfully, and with humor. They ended the class with thumbs up, thumbs down, or thumbs in the middle to asses the effectiveness of their group.

Final reflections

Anita's pre-service program and the two schools where she taught advocated class community, but this only partially explains her success in fostering a dynamic learning community. She is guided by a vision for her class that extends far beyond completing the mandated curriculum expectations. She truly sees teaching as a relational act between herself and the students and between herself and the other teachers, and she believes in students supporting each other's learning and well-being. She also understands the links between program planning and community building: her program supports the growth of community and the strong community allows her to offer an engaging program. Her sunny disposition, her warm manner, her clear understanding of the role of the teacher, her thoughtfulness in all her interactions, her willingness to learn from others, her high expectations for the pupils, her effective classroom management strategies, her efforts to involve parents in their children's schooling, her engaging curriculum, her wisdom about life, and her commitment to her students are all elements that contribute to her class becoming a community.

What and why of classroom organization and community

The aspect of teaching we are considering in this chapter has several sub-elements, including rules, routines, class values, student groupings, classroom management, class community, and the teacher–student relationship, but we believe they are closely connected. For example, as we saw in Anita's profile, a well-organized classroom facilitates community building and a close community in turn provides a basis for effective class activities. Again, students need an overall sense of community membership in order to work well in small groups, but equally as they work in small groups they get to know each other better and the class community is strengthened.

The class culture is so important because the classroom is where most learning occurs and where students spend most of the school day. The character of the overall school setting is also significant, but in part because it determines what is possible in the classroom. At the elementary level especially, the classroom is a large component of students' universe, and the nature of their experience there is vital to their personal well-being and growth. Wanda commented on the importance of this aspect of schooling:

> [F]or me, as a grade 1 teacher, success is having a student or a student's parents tell me that they want to be at school by 7:30 because they want to be the first one in the class. That tells me that hopefully I'm doing something right in terms of creating a nurturing and safe environment and encouraging them to want to learn and love books and just enjoy school.

Dewey (1916) stressed the role of the classroom environment: "We never educate directly, but indirectly by means of the environment" (p. 32). Although the physical surroundings are also important, Dewey was referring here primarily to the social, cultural, and intellectual dimensions of the classroom. These include the teaching program but go beyond it to elements such as the daily schedule, how students are seated together, social relationships in the class, and the general atmosphere. Almost every aspect of how the classroom is run is part of the "environment" and has an impact on students, positively or negatively.

Academic learning should not be our sole concern as we address the classroom context. It is not enough to create a *learning* community, in the sense of a setting for cognitive growth; we must also build a learning *community*, characterized by genuine social and emotional experience. Young people today spend so much of their life in school that it is inappropriate – even abusive, one might say – to restrict this captive population to a narrow band of academic learning. So much else is important and should be attended to in school (Martin, 1992; Noddings, 2005; Peterson, 1992). Zemelman, Daniels, and Hyde (1998) maintain that "the socioemotional development of the classroom community" is a key concern in teaching (p. 192).

Moreover, it is not just social and emotional *learning* that is at issue but the *well-being* of students. The classroom should, among other things, be a place where students feel safe and respected. This is necessary for learning, enabling students to take the risks needed to learn new outlooks and behaviors. But it should also be a major goal in its own right. Again as Dewey (1916) said, education is not just preparation for life, it *is* life; and students are entitled to experience well-being in the present even while a foundation is being laid for the future. In fact, according to Dewey, learning to live well in the present is the best way to learn how to live in the future: the future grows out of the present.

Finally, attending to classroom organization and community is essential for the well-being of the *teacher*. Teachers must be able to survive, remain strong, and indeed enjoy what they do – despite the rigors of teaching – and this is much more likely to occur if they work in a friendly and well-functioning classroom. As Felicity said at the end of her third year of teaching:

> Now that I've done it a few times, I'm looking for ways to make teaching easier without compromising the level of interest and activity in the classroom . . . I'm also looking to enjoy myself more in the classroom. So, I have to figure out how I can do that. How can I make it so it's less stressful for me, and less exhausting, but the children are still getting quality teaching? And I think, really, that breaks down into organization and classroom management, those two. If you can get those two going, then you can really save yourself a lot of stress.

Problems of classroom organization and community

The area of classroom organization and community is beset by many challenges. One frequently mentioned by the new teachers in our study was that they did not know how to implement small-group learning in the classroom: how to make it effective and how to keep students on task. A particular difficulty was the implementation of "guided reading," in which the teacher works with one small group while the rest of the class engages in other group activities. In February of her second year, Maria said:

[With guided reading], time is still an issue . . . What I need to do is sit down and organize centers . . . because the students have to be doing something while you're doing guided reading. And I have an idea what I want the centers to be, but you need to introduce one center a week and have them practice it: it's a process. And I just haven't had time to do all that.

By the end of that second year, Maria reported that she finally had her centers "up and running" and was able to do "a little bit of guided reading in that environment." But she said it had taken a lot of explicit training of the students: "Here's what you're doing. You're at this center. Here's what you don't do. You don't come and disrupt me when I'm conferencing." Karen, on the other hand, still had substantial difficulties with group work toward the end of her third year. It should be noted, however, that she previously taught special education students: this was her first year with a regular class.

I would like my reading groups to be more organized, I would like to have things set out so it's easier for them to do it. Like today, for example, I thought they knew what to do and they didn't; but it's so hard to get the instructions across to three different groups of kids without having them on the carpet for an hour. So a goal of mine is to find a way to do that more efficiently, in a more organized way, so they don't feel so frustrated and I don't feel so frustrated.

Part of the difficulty was that most of the new teachers had not experienced much group work in their own schooling and so did not fully understand its purpose or how to do it: their "apprenticeship" was in a different approach to teaching (Lortie, 1975). Further, in their pre-service program this deficiency was not always addressed adequately. Though small-group learning was constantly mentioned, its purpose was often not explained clearly enough: it tended to be promoted as a slogan or "catch term" (as one of the new teachers said). Anita felt more detail should have been given in pre-service on how to do group work (or alternatives):

[T]he pre-service program [didn't provide] enough practical knowledge . . . Like what's an alternative to literature circles? Because those things work great if you don't have many behavior kids. But if you have a lot of animosity within your class and haven't been able to build a strong community yet, how can you still make things meaningful for them and make it enjoyable *without* [group work]?

It is interesting that although Anita is a strong believer in community (as we saw earlier), she does not think group work is always beneficial: it depends on the circumstances in the class. Accordingly, she wanted to understand not only how to do it but when to do it.

Moving beyond group work, a further problem with collaborative, community-oriented classroom arrangements generally is that even when teachers and students enjoy them, they may not see them as "real school." Again because of their "apprenticeship," there is a tendency to feel that class community – with a truly social emphasis – is too "flaky" to be regarded as an essential part of schooling. Such attitudes place a yet heavier burden on teachers and teacher educators to find ways to explain – and *show* – convincingly why this approach is indeed crucial.

A major challenge reported by the new teachers was disruptive behavior. Interestingly, our study participants on the whole were able to keep order in their classroom: things rarely got out of hand. But the behavior problems meant that a lot of time was wasted, certain learning activities were simply not feasible, and the stress level rose for teacher and students alike. Karen noted: "There are two or three students in my class who are just at loggerheads and it's very stressful to be around them." Jeannie in her second year said she now had "a better sense of classroom management" and her guided reading groups were more effective because "I am able to do them more often and with less interruptions"; whereas in the previous year, "because there were a lot of behavior problems, I didn't really know what I was doing . . . [and] guided reading didn't start until December or January." Nina (teaching grade 2) commented:

> [O]ne of the biggest issues I have in my class is behavior . . . . I have one student who's on Ritalin, and when he doesn't take his medication it changes everything. I've got another student who I think is ADHD, but I'm still [in March] trying to have him diagnosed. He simply cannot sit in his seat. I have another child who is ELL and because of his language frustrations and his personality, he's throwing scissors across the room. Behaviorally it has just been a big challenge. So in my literacy program it's very difficult. For example, guided reading, in theory I love . . . [but] in my class it doesn't work."

Principles and strategies of classroom organization and community

The new teachers made considerable progress over the three years in the complex area of group work, classroom management, classroom organization, and class community. Here we present some principles and strategies in this area, drawing on their views and practices along with other sources.

Balance small-group, individual, and whole-class approaches

Despite the challenges noted earlier, *group work* that is well planned and implemented can greatly enhance the effectiveness and enjoyment of learning (Barone and Morrow, 2003; Kohn, 1999; Zemelman et al., 1998). In particular, the use of guided learning methods (Cunningham and Allington, 2007; Fountas and Pinnell, 1999) – in which the teacher works closely with a small group – can be worthwhile: the students enjoy interacting with the teacher, they receive individualized help, and the teacher is able to get to know the students better. In her third year, Jeannie commented that the reading groups were the strongest element in her program because the teaching was so focused. And Carrie, also in her third year, observed:

> I find small group work is really effective because they learn so much from each other, and they get so much confidence from helping each other. And it's not always the same kid who's stronger, they all have particular contributions. I have one girl who is identified as mildly intellectually delayed and struggled in math until we started looking at money, and she's suddenly the expert because she works part-time in a cafeteria. She'll say: "I've finished, let me show you how it's done."

The point about group work, then, is not that it should be avoided but that we should be selective in how and when we implement it (Allington, 2006; Bainbridge and Malicky, 2004; Zemelman et al., 1998). It should not be seen as *the* main teaching arrangement, but rather should be used only where it is clearly beneficial and when the students are ready for it. In December of her first year Tanya, who is a very strong teacher, said: "I haven't been able to set up literacy centers and guided reading groups . . . Some teachers would start these in September, but I wasn't experienced enough to know how to set up these routines without the students having some independent skills."

Indeed, by the end of their third year several of the new teachers had either abandoned guided reading altogether or were using it to a very limited degree; and some said they refused to feel guilty about this since they had found more effective methods. John reported that:

> guided reading has taken a back seat . . . I've been working with the whole class . . . or with their own personal writing . . . and it's amazing, their writing has improved greatly, their reading has become more critical, and their oral expression is very strong.

Vera commented

> We have been doing a lot more shared reading as opposed to guided
> reading and all that stuff. And in my first two years I maybe would
> have felt uncomfortable with that . . . But now I feel I can make those
> decisions with confidence, knowing this is what the kids need.

Marisa said:

> The biggest change this year is I haven't done guided reading . . . And
> I've had moments of feeling guilty about that [but] I've done other
> things; my whole-class lessons have gone really well, and we've done
> more shared reading and individual writing, which I couldn't do in the
> past because guided reading took up so much time.

Use of small groups should be carefully balanced with individual and
whole-class approaches (Bainbridge and Malicky, 2004). *Individual* work is
crucial for a number of reasons (Allington, 2006; Bainbridge and Malicky,
2004), many of which were discussed in previous chapters. For one thing,
students' abilities, interests, needs, and styles vary so much that they must
often be allowed to work on their own (even when *sitting* in groups). Further, students need practice in taking charge of their own learning, becoming proactive in assessing their strengths and weaknesses and building their
knowledge and skills. Individual learning is also necessary so students can
figure out what interests them and the direction they want their life to
take (Gardner, 1999). In general, students must move beyond being passive
recipients of knowledge and see learning as something *they* do for their
own reasons, not just something done *to* them.

Many of the participants in our study supported an emphasis on individual learning. Anita observed that individual assignments are often necessary
if students are to work effectively while seated in groups. Paul commented
that part of his approach to teaching is:

> getting students going with responsibility, making them responsible for
> their own learning . . . [I say to them] it's your choice, in the end you've
> got to make the decision . . . If you're not good at spelling I can help
> you, but you have to figure out ways you can fix it yourself, or other
> places you can go for help, because I'm not always going to be here.

Wanda said: "I've been trying to refine my approach and . . . allow students
to have a bit more independence in terms of their own learning."

Whole-class activities are also very important (Kohn, 1999; Zemelman
et al., 1998). They provide variety, and are sometimes more engaging than

individual and small-group activities. Students like to get to know others in their class and hear what they have to say; and they like to feel they belong to the larger group. Whole-class work can be easier for the teacher to manage, and it can be a more effective method of teaching certain topics. Further, whole-class activities play a crucial role in community building (Peterson, 1992). Zemelman et al. (1998) maintain that whole-class activities are necessary to build "a productive, interdependent, cooperative classroom community," noting that "if the climate isn't right, small groups will fail" (p. 192). However, they add that if whole-class activities are to have this effect, they must go beyond mere "presentations and instructions" by the teacher and involve "genuine interchange and decision making by students" (p. 192). Kohn (1999) makes a similar point:

> Some progressive educators are understandably suspicious of the whole-class format because in most classrooms that means the teacher runs the show . . . But it is possible for a class to meet for an authentic exchange of ideas in which students address one another directly.
>
> (p. 154)

Among our study participants, Paul in his second year spoke of the importance of whole-class activities. "Because of all the [behavior] problems [this year], I've been doing more on just getting the whole class on the same page and working together." Candice felt not enough attention was given to whole-class work in her pre-service program. She said:

> I would have liked to have more resources [from pre-service] that are acceptable to multiple levels . . . You need to find ideas where everybody can come in and do something with it, including the ELL students and gifted students at the other end.

Nina described the interaction and learning she was able to foster at a whole-class level in her grade 2 class:

> We have a [whole-class] sharing circle every day after independent reading time . . . where everybody takes a turn orally communicating that "I've chosen this book. This is what I found interesting." . . . At the beginning of the year it was very basic, "I like the drawings," but now they're saying "I like the drawings because of the colors they used, the expression on their faces." So I can see the development.

Karen, teaching a combined grade 2/3 class in her third year, said: "I like whole-group work because we're like a big family coming together, and that's where we share a lot of things."

Limit use of ability grouping

When teachers do employ small groups, on what basis should they be formed? We agree with researchers who maintain that using ability as the criterion is a questionable practice (Atwell, 1998; Peterson and Hittie, 2003). According to Zemelman et al. (1998): "One of the signal contributions of educational research has been the explicit rejection of tracking and the affirmation of heterogeneous grouping" (p. 258). A common argument for ability grouping is that less able students feel more comfortable in a separate group, but in fact placing students in a lower group usually makes them feel *less* comfortable overall. Ability grouping undermines students' self-esteem and builds barriers rather than community in a class (Atwell, 1998).

Moreover, research suggests that ability grouping is not sound even from an academic point of view (Atwell, 1998; Cunningham and Allington, 2007). More able students usually do no better academically when grouped together (Bainbridge and Malicky, 2004), and less able students do significantly worse because expectations (both theirs and their teacher's) are lowered and they have less exposure to "more skilled performances" (Darling-Hammond, 1997, p. 131). Cunningham and Allington (2007) state that there is no research whatever to support the view that "within-class groupings according to level" have "long-term effectiveness in accelerating the literacy development of struggling readers" (p. 200). They advocate *multilevel instruction*, an approach that "contains multiple things to be learned and allows all students to feel successful" (p. 200).

Some of the new teachers in our study employed ability grouping, especially for literacy activities. We believe this was partly because they were introduced to it in pre-service as a sound approach and then pressured to use it in their school and school district. However, others said they largely avoided ability grouping. For example, Paul remarked: "I like to do things in groups [but] I think it's important to switch the groups, not to have the same groups all year, and give the students a bit of say in the groups." Tanya reported moving away from ability grouping in her second year:

> In no way do my [grade 4] students identify themselves with somebody else as being at their reading level . . . In grade 1 [last year] the students for the Snuggle Up program took home leveled books to read and they identified themselves as "I am a level F reader and I want to be a level G reader." . . . Whereas here anybody can pick up any book they're motivated to read and read it. I'm loving being away from the leveled reader syndrome.

In the third year, Marisa noted that she had stopped using leveled texts, and Carrie said: "I do ability grouping a little bit but I think their abilities are really mixed . . . I don't necessarily ability-group in terms of cognitive capacity, it's more behavior and things like whether a group will work well together."

Develop effective approaches to group work (small-group or whole-class)

Some of the prejudice against group work among teachers and students is due to the (in our view mistaken) belief that direct presentation of information – without much discussion – is the most efficient teaching method. Many people assume that material presented is material learned, even though this is frequently not the case. Sometimes student teachers will say: "Let's not have all these activities; just tell us how to teach and let us go home early." However, often the negative views toward collaborative work are justly earned because it is poorly conceived and implemented. It is used because it is the latest fad, or to fill in time, or because it keeps students "active." If we are to employ group work responsibly – and convince our students and others of its value – we must figure out how to do it well. This requires sound general principles and a repertoire of effective methods.

Regarding general principles, Cossey and Tucher (2005) raise the question "What will make a collaborative effort worth your while?" and go on to suggest some key principles (pp. 116–117):

- ask yourself if the project . . . is sufficiently complex and interesting
- consider whether each individual [in the group] has something in particular to do
- [ask whether group members] hold a diversity of perspectives
- ask . . . whether a collaborative effort is worth your time [on this occasion].

Other principles could be added, such as:

- explain to students the purposes of group work
- train students over time in particular group methods
- provide clear instructions for an activity, often in writing
- choose a group size that matches the task and age level (usually, the younger the students the smaller the group)
- vary the group methods used (both to heighten interest and to enable more students to get to know each other),

The central question underlying many of these principles is: *What will the students learn from this group activity, and why will they learn it better through group work than other methods?* Sometimes, of course, we may opt for a group activity even when it will not be more effective for academic learning, whether to build class community or simply to add variety to the class experience. But effectiveness for student learning must always be a major consideration.

With respect to particular collaborative methods (small-group or whole-class), many are described in the literature: Bainbridge and Malicky (2004, pp. 443–445); Cunningham and Allington (2007, pp. 182–200); Grossman and Schoenfeld (2005, pp. 224–227); Kohn (1999, pp. 153–156); and Zemelman et al. (1998, pp. 189–193). Examples include:

- peer tutoring, assessing, and editing
- working in twos and threes
- think, pair, share (often a three-stage process from the individual to the whole class)
- guided learning (in which a small group works with the teacher)
- literature circles (such as book clubs)
- learning centers (different activities in different locations around the room)
- group projects (in which the group develops a product together)
- "jigsaw" activities (in which discussion preparation tasks are divided among group members)
- whole-class discussion
- whole-class debates
- simply going around the room (with the opportunity to "pass").

Many of these activities work well in combination: for example, jigsaw activities followed by reporting back to the whole class. In a class where a few students tend to dominate whole-class discussion (which is nearly always the case), some of the above methods can be used to reduce this problem.

Build community in the classroom

A major condition for successful small-group and whole-class learning is to have a strong class community. The pedagogical literature supports the notion that community in the classroom is not just a frill: it is fundamental to effective learning. Peterson (1992) states: "When community exists, learning is strengthened – everyone is smarter, more ambitious, and productive" (p. 2). According to Dewey (1938), "education is essentially a social process. This quality is realized in the degree in which individuals form a community group" (p. 58). Vygotsky (1978) maintained that human language and interactions convey many implicit messages. Even if students wished to, they could not live in their own bubble in the classroom. The class milieu continually impinges on their thoughts, emotions, and relationships, imposing certain meanings on the messages they receive from the teacher and other sources. Accordingly, the form that milieu takes is of vital importance.

Class community supports academic learning, but it has significance far beyond that. As discussed earlier, it is essential to students' personal well-being and their social and emotional development. Moreover, it is crucial for the well-being of the teacher, who must live day in and day out with the class. Indeed, our work both in schools and pre-service programs has led us to the view that genuine community in the classroom is the single most important factor in successful teaching (Beck and Kosnik, 2001; Beck and Kosnik, 2006). Teachers should spend a significant proportion of their time directly or indirectly building community.

Anita's profile, reviewed earlier, showed clearly the importance she attaches to community building and the positive impact it has on her class. Many other new teachers in our study supported this emphasis, outlining some of the strategies they use to foster community. For example, Wanda said:

> I try to incorporate some of the Tribes approach: the concept of building community, building a team, and understanding that we have to respect one another and have kindness and trust in the classroom. Together we sit down and look at the type of classroom rules we want, what we expect of one another, and the importance of listening attentively to each other. And that was a theme throughout the year . . . They got tired of hearing me say that the more friends you have the better off you are.

John reported:

> [E]very day we have a community circle where the students sit in a circular fashion, facing me and each other, and we go around . . . And there are rules of course, the right to pass and so on . . . it makes them feel safe.

Carrie in her third year commented: "I've done a lot of talking around how I expect to be treated and how they should expect to be treated, and why; and about how it's okay to express opinions about things, but it's how you say it." Nina, also in her third year, described how she focuses on

> four tenets: cooperation, kindness, honesty, and choices . . . and I work with those words and have them understand them deeply. And I make it clear there is no tolerance for laughing at each other, no tolerance for bullying . . . And if there's a problem at recess, I say "I can't believe that someone in my class would do that." . . . So I think that within my

classroom, most of the children feel safe and that they can be themselves, and we work as a team for the most part.

Take a broad approach to classroom management

Good classroom management is a crucial aspect of classroom life, necessary both for learning and for student and teacher well-being. We saw earlier many of the challenges our new teachers faced in this area, resulting in considerable stress, time wasted, and inability to implement certain learning activities. However, trying to manage a class through rules alone is not viable. Many teachers today are experimenting with a "zero-tolerance" approach to classroom management, instituting a detailed rule system and stopping the class almost every time a rule is broken. But on the whole this approach is not working. Students lose interest when learning activities are constantly interrupted and the focus shifts from learning to trying to outmaneuver the teacher. Also, animosity builds between teacher and students.

In our view, classroom management is inseparable from everything else we have been discussing in this book and chapter. Success in this area involves working on many fronts at once (Evertson, Emmer, and Worsham, 2006; LePage, Darling-Hammond, and Akar, 2005). For example, it requires:

- well-chosen topics of study that as far as possible interest students, engage them, connect to their lives, and meet their individual learning needs
- a variety of effective learning activities
- understood ways of doing things in the classroom, so students know what is expected
- firmness on the part of the teacher (as we saw with Anita): quick action where needed
- kindness on the part of the teacher (again as we saw with Anita): acting with humor, care, and interest in the students as human beings
- a strong class community that students enjoy, and within which they see themselves as valued members who also have responsibility for other members – including the teacher.

The participants in our study came from their pre-service preparation with many useful ideas about classroom management and they soon added new ones. Felicity observed that if you "keep it interesting . . . that helps with your classroom management." Vera talked about the need to balance firmness with friendliness in relating to students. She said she wishes she had been told (in pre-service) "how to maintain a positive climate while keeping structure – how to be fun without being unkind or mean"; she wishes she had known "that the students won't hate me for being firm." Wanda spoke of the role of the community in classroom management:

I believe in creating a sense of community in my class so the students understand that, yes, they are individuals but they are also part of a larger unit, and they have to work together and everybody has to support each other in order to be successful.

Similarly, Paul described how he relies on class dynamics to help with classroom management:

There are students who are really good at class "citizenship": belonging to the community, getting along, finding solutions to problems; and there are other students who are not good at that at all. But a few students at the lower end have definitely developed some skills in this area over the year. It's just like if you live in a small town . . . eventually they accept you because . . . you're all they have . . . And I've seen a few students really shine: they know what to say to people and how to get the whole class calmed down or listening or doing what they're supposed to.

Develop a close teacher–student relationship

A close relationship between teacher and students is a crucial piece in classroom organization and community. According to Dewey (1938), "[i]t is absurd to exclude the teacher from membership in the [class] group" (p. 58). Teachers have to take the lead in establishing the community: setting up communal structures, speaking explicitly about the importance of community, and modeling the kinds of attitudes and relationships that are essential to community-oriented education. Rightly or wrongly, *teachers are key figures in educational settings*: they are charged with establishing the agenda, setting the tone, and making final decisions about what is acceptable. Accordingly, they must be fully and personally involved in something as comprehensive and complex as forming a class community (Kosnik and Beck, 2003).

This emphasis on the role of the teacher does not, in our opinion, imply a top-down conception of community or undermine notions of democracy, constructivism, and student ownership of their learning. It is simply that the teacher's status in the classroom means that movement in a democratic, constructivist direction is inconceivable unless the teacher is fully on board. As Felicity said:

With the atmosphere in your classroom, you really have to start from the top. You need to be positive and create that atmosphere in yourself, and that is what your classroom will be like . . . You have to decide, what kind of classroom do I want to be in, and would I like to be in as a student?

The teacher must model warmth and affection in the community (Martin, 1992; Noddings, 2005). Our students are not our "friends" in the ordinary sense, but we must be friendly toward them. Without a social and emotional dimension, we have at most a collaborative learning group, not a genuine community. If the teacher remains a largely detached "instructor," focused mainly on academic success and uninterested in students' idiosyncrasies and personal needs, the sense of community in the classroom will be minimal. The teacher's academic role is very important, but it must not be the only one. Jody, who in year 3 was working with special needs students, said:

> I'm guided by the thought, Imagine going to a place where you fail every day. And these kids do . . . So I always try to be supportive. I push them as much as I can to get them to learn, but I do it in a really positive way.

Paul spoke about the kind of interplay of personal and academic elements needed in the classroom:

> [W]hen you tell a student, "You need to stop doing that, you need to do this, you need to learn that, you need to do your homework," if they really have no relationship with you – or the relationship is negative – they're not going to follow what you say. And my students, some more than others, when I say something they listen because it's like, "Oh yeah, that person, I respect what they say and that person is honest and honorable. So I will believe what they say." It sounds old-fashioned but I think it's really true. And we talk a lot about respect in school but honestly not a ton of it gets shown toward students. Teachers demand respect but some of the ways they treat students are not respectful and the students know it.

Along these lines, Nina said:

> I need to use respectful language and treat each child with respect. Because if they see me more in a kind of master–slave relationship, how can I expect them to treat the other students – and me – with respect?

Emphasize inclusion and equity

All the aspects of classroom dynamics discussed so far – productive small-group and whole-class work, strong class community, effective classroom management, and a good teacher–student relationship – are in turn dependent on respecting students' diverse personalities and backgrounds. Without such respect students will not be inclined to collaborate with one another, participate in the class community, or like and trust their teacher. Respect for students has many aspects, but a key one is respecting racial, ethnic, gender, and other differences and ensuring that all students feel accepted in the class community. How to foster such respect and acceptance will be discussed at some length in Chapter 4.

In focusing on diversity and inclusion, however, we should be wary of stereotyping, which can quickly undermine community. Irvine (2003) observes that "inadequate or cursory knowledge can lead to more, not less, hostility and stereotyping toward culturally different students" (p. 16). Melnick and Zeichner (1997) report that "at times, teacher education practices designed to combat negative stereotypes actually reinforce teacher candidates' prejudices and misconceptions about diverse students" (p. 29). There should be much discussion in class of the fact that diversity exists more within groups than between them, and that people from different groups have many more commonalities than differences. Irvine (2003) stresses the need to foster awareness of "the shared interests and connections of all people in the world," as well as the differences (p. 17), and this is obviously important for a strong class community.

Implications for pre-service education

We have suggested that classroom organization and community building are among the most important factors in effective teaching. But in practice they tend to be neglected in pre-service programs: in particular, the role of the class community often receives little attention. What can be done to enhance pre-service preparation in this area?

Emphasize class community and the social and emotional aspects of teaching and learning

The most important step in this direction is to build community in the pre-service program itself. This involves structuring the students into cohort groups, each with its own faculty team, as we have described elsewhere (Beck and Kosnik, 2006). Once we have the cohorts, social interaction can be fostered through retreats, whole-class discussion, group work in class, group assignments, getting-to-know-you activities in class, social gatherings in homes and other locations, exchanges on an internet conference dedicated to personal and social matters, and having students clustered as much as possible in their practicum placements. Given the pressure on teacher education today to "cover" a great deal of material, one may wonder how time can be found for social activities. However, in our view there is no alternative: embodying social and emotional learning in pre-service programs is essential if we are to convince student teachers of its importance and teach them how to foster it themselves. Of course, against the background of modeling a social emphasis we should also spend a considerable amount of time in class discussing the importance of this emphasis and strategies for building community.

Emphasize the teacher–student relationship

If genuine community is to emerge in a pre-service cohort, the faculty team must participate in the social activities, in many cases taking the lead in organizing them. Most student teachers are extremely busy, and given their previous apprenticeship in un-social forms of education, they are unlikely to change their approach unless the faculty show very clearly their commitment to social and emotional learning. Also, they will be reluctant to appear too keen in such matters in front of their peers. Apart from facilitating the social side, it is important for faculty to show a genuine interest in talking socially with the students and getting to know them as people. This models the kind of teacher–student relationship we have said is so important in the school classroom. Unless teachers find ways to transcend a purely formal relationship, many important opportunities for teachers and students to learn from each other will be lost.

Integrate instruction about classroom organization, class community, and pedagogy

Whereas class community tends to be neglected in pre-service programs, classroom management usually receives a lot of attention, as of course does pedagogy. With regard to classroom organization the situation is mixed: it is discussed to some extent, but key aspects are overlooked. We propose that ways be found to emphasize all these topics and integrate their study as much as possible. As noted in an earlier section, classroom management cannot be achieved in isolation; it is dependent on many factors, including interesting programming, familiar classroom learning structures, and a sense of community in the classroom. And the same is true of other aspects of the teacher's role: they must be pursued together. Given that different instructors are involved, such integration presents a challenge in pre-service programming. Faculty need to work closely together, identifying common principles and goals in this area, writing a handbook for students outlining the program's philosophy, organizing team teaching and other joint activities, farming out topics to ensure the objectives are achieved, and structuring the practicum (e.g., clustered placements) to embody the program emphasis on community.

Adopt a less doctrinaire approach to group work and "guided" teaching

As discussed in earlier sections, a major problem identified by our research was that new teachers left pre-service believing they must immediately implement a great deal of group work in their classroom, including "guided reading," "guided writing," and so forth. They had great difficulty with this initially, and after three years many were not doing guided reading and all were stressing the need for a *balance* between individual, small-group, and whole-class methods. We think that a balance of this kind should be advocated in pre-service – instead of having such a strong emphasis on group work – and more time should be spent discussing when and when not to use the different configurations and how to use them effectively.

Adopt an integrated approach to inclusion and equity

We believe that an inclusive approach to teaching (to be discussed at length in Chapter 4), is fundamental to sound teaching and supports all other aspects of classroom organization and community. However, in pre-service programs inclusion and equity are often addressed as a separate topic, and sometimes by a specialist in this area. We recommend that, as with the other topics discussed in this section, all program faculty become involved in addressing inclusive education, showing in detail its implications for all aspects of teaching and the life of the classroom.

Conclusion

Although program planning and everyday assessment are crucial for pupil learning, equally important is the setting in which the learning occurs. For academic learning, pupils must feel safe and respected in the classroom, and participate in regular learning routines that – as far as possible – they understand and find engaging. For social and emotional growth, pupils must belong to a strong class community in which they can steadily acquire the values and skills of interpersonal living.

In pre-service education today, dividing the class into small groups is strongly emphasized, especially in literacy teaching. In our view, a more balanced approach to classroom organization should be advanced in pre-service, with individual and whole-class methods stressed in addition to small-group work. Further, pre-service programs need to give more attention to the role of the classroom community, with special focus on the teacher–student relationship. Class community should be a major topic of discussion and should be modeled in the pre-service program itself. Cohorts of student teachers should be formed, each with a faculty team, and a variety of processes put in place to ensure that each cohort becomes a strong community.

Chapter 4

Inclusive education

Another priority in teaching and teacher education, closely connected to classroom organization and community, is what we will call "inclusive education." As noted in the previous chapter, feeling respected and accepted is crucial for student participation in classroom life and learning. And beyond such participation, students need to understand the phenomenon of prejudice and discrimination and acquire inclusive outlooks, attitudes, and behavior patterns, both for the school setting and for their life in general.

The concept of inclusion used in this chapter embraces a large set of concepts: equity, social justice, respect for difference, gender equity, multi-culturalism, anti-racism, academic mainstreaming, and so on. We believe a comprehensive approach to this area is needed because prejudice and discrimination of all kinds have a strongly negative impact on people's lives and on society. Adopting such a broad approach to inclusive education is in line with much current writing in the field (Ainscow, Booth, and Dyson, 2006; Melnick and Zeichner, 1997; Verma, Bagley, and Jha, 2007).

All the new teachers in our study came from pre-service programs with a heavy emphasis on inclusion, and almost all were teaching in schools with a student body diverse in race, ethnicity, economic status, and academic achievement. In our interviews, we asked the teachers about their views and practices with respect to "diversity and equity." Most of them noted the attention paid to such topics in their pre-service program and strongly endorsed this emphasis.

We begin the chapter with a profile of Paul, who seemed to us to have exceptionally strong insights and practices in this area.

Paul

> I have kids who have seen people getting shot, they've seen people being stabbed, they've seen lots of drug dealing and prostitution with their own eyes, regularly. So these kids have a different point of view.

Background

Paul came to teaching after spending eight years as an architect. Having immigrated from Korea with his family at an early age, he had been involved in his youth in the local Korean community where his father was a minister. He taught both Sunday school and violin to members of his church; although very musical, he did not consider pursuing a degree or career in music. His first three years of teaching after completing his credential program were in an extremely high-needs urban school where all the children live in subsidized or low-rent apartments. As the opening quote indicates, many of his students do not have "traditional" life experiences.

Paul's school, with approximately 550 children, aims to build community and reach out to the community. Many students belong to visible minority groups, many are English Language Learners (ELLs), and a high proportion are designated as special needs. Such diversity is attractive to Paul, who has a strong commitment to public schooling. In a year 3 interview he commented:

> For me, public education is very important . . . I think segregating people at too young an age in a culture is just not good. Even if it's harder to have them together, and even if they do not excel as much academically, the benefits far outweigh the costs . . . I don't think being powerful and rich is as important as culture. I would actually rather live in a poorer country where people get along . . . I want people to have a good quality of life and help each other have a good quality of life, even if it means they drive a Honda rather than a BMW.

For the first two years Paul taught grade 5, and in his third year he taught a class for "learning disabled" students. As a former ELL student himself, he feels he can relate to some of the challenges his students face.

Obviously, Paul's undergraduate degree in architecture did not have direct relevance to teaching children; however, he feels his work experience "helped because I had a job where things were complicated and changed a lot. You're always talking with people and communicating. With architecture obviously there's a lot of creativity and invention, so I could transfer those skills to teaching." Paul was fairly positive about his one-year pre-service program in which he received his credential to teach kindergarten through grade 6, although he did note some shortcomings. The cohort program he chose was

> focused on inner-city schools, it was definitely tailored to that demographic. I got a lot of great ideas about books and resources that have been really useful. I got suggestions for how to structure things so as to be flexible and responsive to the students' backgrounds.

He found his two practice teaching placements helpful, one in grade 2 and one in a combined grade 4/5/6 class (in an alternative school). He wished his pre-service program had focused more on assessment and on theories of how children develop as readers and writers. He also felt some of the assignments were simply "busy work."

Description of practice

At the heart of Paul's practice is a commitment to helping his students succeed. Attention to equity, diversity, and developing an inclusive community are the foundation of his work as a teacher, not simply "add-ons" to his program. He defines diversity broadly as including race, gender, class, and academic ability. Paul's own experience of racism growing up, his reading on social justice, and his involvement in a support group for Gay, Lesbian, and Transgendered parents have given him an in-depth understanding of many related issues. His recognition of the links between education and overcoming societal barriers has led him to develop a program to help students acquire the knowledge, skills, and attitudes – in particular the self-esteem – to achieve in society and become involved citizens.

Believing that teaching is a relational act, Paul spends time getting to know his students: what is going on in their lives, their interests, anxieties, and strengths. "Teaching is a social skill; not just the performance aspect, but actually having relationships with people and developing those relationships." A natural extension of this position is to create a strong and safe class community. At the beginning of the school year he devotes time to community, using strategies such as daily sports activities, building Lego structures in groups, and talking about community. Given the life context of many of the children, Paul wants the class to be a place where they can raise questions. He aims to build a high trust level with his students, which was evident when one of his students said to him: Is it normal to want to punch your mom? "My reaction was not panicky, even though inside I'm going, Whoa! My reply was, Well, that's an interesting question. Why don't we talk about that later on? I think it's really important for kids to feel they can speak about things."

In designing his literacy program, Paul wants to make connections with the real world and help children see that literacy is all around them.

> School has to connect to their real world, even if it is violent. Our students are jaded in a way, they are immature but they're also too worldly. I find I need things that are real-world, high-interest. But it's hard to find those things because a lot are not appropriate for school, or not deemed appropriate. Most of the music these kids listen to you can't listen to at school. I find that weird in a way, because what does that mean? They come to school and everything they like to do – the

games, the music – they are not allowed to do at school. I find it worrisome that school is becoming irrelevant to them. Is it becoming so removed from their "real life" that they don't care about it?

He finds using newspapers a good strategy to make literacy relevant: the variety of sections appeals to a range of interests, articles are short, and the pictures help with comprehension. With multiple copies of the paper available, students often sit in groups reading and discussing the paper. He described one such session and commented: "They had this appearance of adult men sitting around, reading the paper, chatting about politics and sports. It was kind of neat to see that." Paul finds that graphic novels help make text accessible to his students. His students use computers effectively and he often books the school computer lab for his class. He thinks students need to be computer literate if they are to have a chance to succeed.

Paul promotes inclusion in part through the books he uses in his literacy program. He reads aloud to his students every day, often from books that address issues of equity and diversity. One of the novels he read to his students was

> *The Jacket*, about a boy who accuses another boy of stealing, and the boy who gets accused happens to be Black. It's all about racism, internalized racism, etc. It was a really good book, short, easy to get into. And the kids were just on the edge of their seats. [A second book I read], *The Breadwinner*, is about a girl living in Afghanistan during the Taliban occupation. So again, it was really interesting, connected to the students.

Paul was introduced to many books dealing with race, class, and gender in his pre-service program and continues to use them: for example, *Are You a Boy or a Girl?*, *Deshawn Days*, *Dreamcatcher*, *Heather Has 2 Mommies*, *Let's Talk about Race*, *Sticks and Stones* (about internet bullying), and *Zen Shorts*. He both reads aloud to students and encourages them to read on their own. "I had a girl who was very, very boyish and she read *Are You a Boy or a Girl?* I would see her reading it and she was processing it and going, Oh, it's okay that I'm not so girlish." In addition to this literature-based approach, Paul discusses inclusion explicitly with students when they make racist or ethnocentric comments in the classroom. He said: "I know that's what they hear at home, that some families are really racist . . . so I don't feel I can change their beliefs right away; but I want to show them what's acceptable and that they can't get away with saying things like that in class."

Sometimes Paul teaches skills in discrete lessons and at other times integrated into content areas. From his first year of teaching, Paul has tended to blur curriculum boundaries. When doing a social studies unit on early civilizations, he integrates "reading, comprehension, research skills, writing, sentences, paragraphs, and writing reports." He feels linking skills and content makes the program more engaging while also allowing him to attend to the many official curriculum expectations. Paul is not a teacher who feels pressure to "get through the curriculum"; rather, he aims to increase his students' understanding and expand their horizons. He wants to introduce students to many genres (especially the boys who only want to read books about sports) and encourages them to be self-directed, motivated, and responsible for their learning. He spends countless hours searching the internet and the library for resources. He feels that almost every resource has to be modified or tailored for his students. He complains about some of the items on the standardized test he has to administer because they revolve around a story about a cottage. As he notes, most of his students have never been to a cottage and have no concept of "going to the cottage."

Part of Paul's understanding of diversity is awareness that the cultures of many of his students are fairly oral and that oral language can be a bridge to print.

> I started a storytelling club this year and I do storytelling with my kids. I realized that a lot of kids need to be able to speak clearly, put their ideas together, and *say* them before they can even put them down. If they can't string together a sentence orally they're probably not going to sit down and write a coherent sentence. For a lot of these kids, oral language is huge. You can tell them a story and they will remember so much, but they will read the story on paper and remember and understand much less.

Paul's class in action

There are nine in Paul's class for "learning disabled" students (the class he had in his third year) – all boys, some with severe behavior issues, three students from each of grades 4, 5, and 6. From the moment the children tumble through the doorway, energy fills the room. The classroom is fairly small, with desks arranged in groups, a sofa, large arm chairs, and workspaces. Paul notes that it takes his students a long time to complete a task and he works patiently with them.

The afternoon begins with a review of how to write a summary for a story. It is difficult for the group to focus but Paul gently reminds them to attend to the lesson. After a short lesson the students read trade books, either *The Salamander Room* or *Demolition* (a non-fiction text on techniques for demolishing buildings). Some students choose to read independently while others read with a partner. Some sit at their desks, others on the sofa, and one student who is known to like to read on his own without being disturbed sits apart in one of the easy chairs. It is interesting to observe the students because the more able ones help those struggling with decoding or comprehension.

The students reading *Demolition* so enjoy the book that they want to read beyond the assigned chapters, which Paul allows them to do. He chose the book because many of the government-subsidized units where the children live are being torn down: they are literally being demolished before the students' eyes. As they read, students talk about the apartments being ripped down, the noise, the dust, and their concern about where they will live.

After a recess break, the students continue writing their summaries. Some use the computer program *Co-Writer*, which speaks the text as it is being written and gives choices for words as the students begin to spell them. It is a very good program and the students like using it. As they complete their summaries the students begin work on their art, which Paul is going to submit to the school-wide art fair. Some work on sketches, some start painting; they chat as they work, sharing materials and assisting each other. As the end of the school day nears, Paul helps the pupils organize their materials for home and tidy up. He reminds them, with a great deal of humor, to remember to return to school tomorrow! He lets students take home computer disks (CD-ROMs) for computer programs they like to use.

Final thoughts

Over the three years, Paul's skills as a teacher have improved – for example, in program planning – but the challenges he faces on a daily basis have rarely ebbed. The needs of the children are so great and their behavior at times so extreme that teaching drains him, as it would any teacher. Without a doubt his students' literacy and social skills improve, but at what cost to him personally?

Paul may see himself as a role model for his students but we also see him as a role model for teacher educators. We recognize that his teacher education program, focusing on urban schools, supported the development of his teaching skills, introduced him to a wide range of resources, and helped him refine his vision for schooling. The marrying of pedagogy and vision helped him become a truly outstanding practitioner. However, teacher educators cannot take all the credit: Paul is a truly remarkable individual with distinctive life experiences, talents, and insights. Teacher education needs to continue to attract candidates like Paul, and the school system needs to support committed young professionals so they remain in teaching, keeping intact their vision for supporting youth of diverse backgrounds.

What and why of inclusive education

Paul's profile illustrates the comprehensive approach to inclusive education mentioned earlier. In his classroom, he addresses matters of race, ethnicity, language, poverty, ability, gender, and sexual orientation. He is concerned not only to critique prejudice and discrimination but also to help disad-vantaged students acquire academic skills, a love of learning, a positive self-concept, and direction for the future. As Melnick and Zeichner (1997) say, "an adequate definition of 'diversity' needs to be broad and inclusive." These authors focus especially on "social class, race, ethnicity, and lan-guage," but they maintain that attention must also be given to "gender, age, religion, exceptionalities, sexual orientation, etc." (p. 25).

In earlier decades, the term "inclusive education" usually referred to the practice of placing "special education" students – that is, students with "learning disabilities" – in mainstream classrooms. However, the broader usage we favor is now becoming more common. Verma et al. (2007) observe that:

> [A] plethora of critical literature has emerged recently, re-examining the concept of inclusive education from an educational reform per-spective. Schools in this critical perspective should respond and adapt to the needs of *all* children, regardless of gender, physical, cognitive and sensory needs, ethnicity and religious and cultural background, and fit themselves to children's learning styles and needs, and not the other way round.
>
> (pp. 33–34)

Similarly, Ainscow et al. (2006) state that, in keeping with a trend that is emerging "internationally," the aim of inclusion in education is "to reduce exclusion and discriminatory attitudes, including those in relation to age, social class, ethnicity, religion, gender and attainment" (p. 2).

And the definitional issues do not end there. Even with agreement that inclusive education should be conceived broadly, there remain questions about how we should implement it. For example: (i) we can have separate lessons or units on inclusion, or alternatively "infuse" it into our teach-ing and modeling within subjects, across subjects, and in the life of the classroom; (ii) we can focus mainly on understanding and respecting the differences between students of various racial, ethnic, and other groups, or rather stress commonalities as well as differences; and (iii) we can have a "constructivist" approach to fostering an inclusive outlook, allowing it to emerge in students as they respond to information, discussion, and class-room experiences, or instead impose it "top-down." In later sections we will make a case for an approach that is largely infused into the program, focuses on commonalities as well as differences, and is constructivist rather than top-down in nature.

What is the rationale for viewing inclusive education – in the broad sense just discussed – as a high priority in teaching and hence teacher education? Apart from general ethical and political arguments for treating people equally and humanely, we believe inclusive pedagogy is required by the progressive, constructivist view of teaching that we (along with most other teacher educators) advocate (Beck and Kosnik, 2006). It comes with the territory. We agree with Villegas and Lucas (2002) that "student diversity is central to the learning process" (p. xxii). Inclusion is inherent in a pedagogical approach that emphasizes critical inquiry, recognition of the "other," respect for student experience, student construction of learning, class community, and a close teacher–student relationship. We cannot say we believe in taking students' needs, experience, and point of view seriously and then not support *all* students in the classroom and, less directly, in their lives beyond the school.

As an educational institution, the school is an especially fitting context in which to tackle issues of inclusion, since the opposite of inclusion – prejudice and discrimination – is fed in part by mistaken beliefs. At least two types of mistaken belief are involved: *prejudice* against certain groups, i.e., the false belief that they are inferior; and *stereotyping* of groups, i.e., the false belief that "they are all the same." These are usually not just beliefs, of course, being often in part rationalizations of self-interested behavior; nevertheless, the belief component is high and as such should be addressed by schools as academic institutions.

Finally, teachers have reason to promote inclusion in the classroom because, as noted earlier, student learning depends to a considerable extent on being in an inclusive classroom community. Students need to feel safe, accepted, and respected if they are to be able to concentrate, take risks, and learn. As we saw in Chapter 3, Anita fostered community in her highly multi-racial, multi-ethnic classroom, commenting that "you have to have a strong community in your classroom before any sort of deep learning can take place."

Problems of inclusive education

Despite the value and legitimacy of inclusive education (in the broad sense discussed), it is beset by many challenges. Perhaps the biggest is that it is such a difficult area to understand and address. It is not helpful to suggest, as some people do, that it is quite obvious what is required and we should just get on with it. In reality, the ethical, political, and cultural issues are very complex, and careful analysis is needed if we are to make a convincing case for inclusion and avoid simply reinforcing existing stereotypes. For example, as we said in the previous chapter and will argue further in this one, exploring the commonalities between different groups is a crucial aspect of inclusive pedagogy, and this requires a great deal of knowledge and pedagogical skill on the part of the teacher.

Another difficulty is that students often bring prejudices, stereotypes, and exclusionary practices to school with them, and questioning these can appear to challenge their basic identity. Initially, trying to promote inclusion in the classroom can in fact give rise to discord as students disagree with each other and with what we are proposing. Paley in her book *You Can't Say You Can't Play* (1992) describes how even kindergarten and early elementary students often have a strong sense that they should be able to choose whom they play with and any attempt by the teacher to take away this choice is an attack on their rights and well-being.

Moreover, inclusive education can lead to tensions and clashes outside the school. Even as pupils move toward adopting more inclusive outlooks and behavior, they need to find ways to continue their respect for – and sense of belonging in – the home and local community. Beyond these local settings, problems can also arise at the larger societal level, where an inclusive outlook may be at odds with traditional nationalistic sentiments: teachers and pupils alike may be seen as adopting an unpatriotic stance.

Yet again, teachers who wish to foster inclusion face challenges arising from the way schooling is conceptualized and organized. Notably, the typical school curriculum is focused on academic learning not directly related to issues of inclusion or to personal, cultural, and political issues generally. Accordingly, it is difficult to find time in the busy school day to deal adequately with such matters (Sleeter, 2005, p. 1). Many students, parents, and politicians – not to mention fellow teachers – do not view study in this area as "real school."

A further problem lies in ability grouping, widely mandated in schools at present (especially for literacy teaching), which tends to support stereotyping and prejudice. Related to this is the withdrawal from the classroom of ELL and special education students far beyond what can be justified on educational grounds. These practices reinforce the exclusion of certain students from full membership in the class community.

Finally, teachers – experienced, new, or in training – often lack experience of diverse settings and sophisticated understanding of issues of inclusion and exclusion. Though typically very sympathetic, they can have prejudices and stereotypes of their own. On the whole, the new teachers in our study had considerable experience of multi-cultural settings. However, they came largely from upper to lower middle-class families and still had much to learn about life in other sectors of society.

Principles and strategies of inclusive education

Although teachers cannot single-handedly cure the ills of society (Kosnik, 1999), there is much they can do to promote inclusion in their classroom and foster the development of their students in this domain. In this section we outline some relevant principles and strategies derived from the research literature and the views and practices of the new teachers in our study.

Emphasize community

Students are strongly influenced by the views of their peers and what they see practiced in their classroom, and this applies in particular to matters of inclusion. As Linda Kroll at Mills College said in an interview:

> If you're going to talk about issues of social justice, equity, and excellence and have hard conversations about things like race and discrimination and how you feel about those things, then you have to have a safe place to talk about it. And if you are going to take risks, showing that you don't know something, there has to be a safe place. So . . . the first thing you have to do is establish a community in your classroom where people feel free to say what they think.
>
> (Beck and Kosnik, 2006, p. 73)

Although Kroll was speaking here primarily about the pre-service context, the same argument applies to the school setting. If pupils are to think and speak freely about issues of inclusion and "try out" inclusive behavior, there has to be genuine community in the classroom.

As noted, nearly all the participants in our study were teaching in schools with considerable diversity of race, ethnicity, economic situation, and academic attainment. One of their main strategies for achieving and teaching inclusion in this context was to build a strong class community. Wanda said she worked at

> creating community, because the biggest issue is getting the children to understand that their uniquenesses are fabulous, but we also need to draw on each other's strengths so we can support each other's weaknesses and create a sense of community.

Jeannie commented:

> I talk a lot about respect – it's actually a school-wide focus – and in September especially I do a lot of activities around it. And I model it: if there is name-calling, I stop the class and address it. And in the read-alouds I talk about bullying, teasing, and so on . . . and about recognizing people's differences and accepting them.

Vera observed:

> I've found that implementing some of the Tribes curriculum into the class has changed the dynamics and reached some students who might otherwise have been isolated. And I think building that kind of inclusion in the classroom makes them want to take more risks in their learning, in literacy and other areas.

Small groups used in teaching often form along ethnic, racial, gender, or class lines, especially if ability grouping is involved; this in turn reinforces labeling and stereotyping. As we noted in Chapter 3, many of the new teachers saw the need to vary the groups and, in particular, avoid ability grouping as much as possible. For example, Sophia reported: "My small groups are heterogeneous from the beginning of the year, because I want everyone to realize that they can learn from others and that everyone has something of value to share." And Tanya said her literacy groups

> are random, they change . . . I tend to have the same text but change the comprehension question, depending on the students I have. And I have students who are really strong in non-fiction but much weaker in fiction and vice versa, so I tend to change the groups depending on the articles I'm reading.

Develop a close teacher–student relationship

As discussed in Chapter 3, the teacher–student relationship is crucial to effective teaching in general; and it is certainly important for inclusive education. Teachers have to set the tone, showing that they respect all the students equally and are genuinely interested in getting to know them all. Martin (1992) maintains that school should be a place where students feel "safe, secure, loved, at ease . . . 'at home'" (p. 12). It should be characterized by "affection . . . intimacy and connection" (p. 18). Deborah Meier (1995), who has been highly successful in establishing and running racially inclusive schools, favors small schools even at the high school level because a large school "takes its staff away from, not toward, its students. Students move about bereft of relationships with anyone but their exact age and grade peers" (p. 113). She continues: "Strong relationships between adults and the young are good for kids. They're more important than all the so-called extras big schools can offer" (p. 114). Sleeter (2005), also speaking of a multi-cultural context, emphasizes the need for teachers to "continually work to get to know their students, both in and out of school, in order to build new learning on what they actually know or find interesting" (p. 108). She says teachers often have "stereotypes about students' lives outside school [that] substitute for knowledge of their lives" (p. 107).

One of the new teachers in our study – Wanda – described the situation in her school with respect to the teacher–student relationship.

> There's a really good relationship, for the most part, between the students and teachers. There's a fine line, with the teachers having the students' respect because they're the teachers but also showing a lot of true concern for the students, and the students liking the teachers as well. So it's a good mix.

Later she explained why it is essential for teachers to get to know their own students well: "I can't say how I'm going to approach anything until I get to know the kids. And I think this is really important, both as a person and as a teacher." Carrie made a particularly poignant comment about the need for a supportive teacher–student relationship:

> I've done more around acceptance of difference this year [year 3] than last year, and also encouraging students to believe in their abilities and accept themselves . . . setting them up with things they can do and tracking the changes . . . My brother has a learning disability and probably my dad does too. So it's always been a core thing with me, that you learn differently, it's not that you can't learn . . . and you've got a right to an education. And also as a child myself I saw what it means to a kid when a teacher condemns them and doesn't support them. And I think, what's the point of being a teacher if you just go in angry and take it out on the kids. Time to get a new job.

Individualize the program

If we are to show respect toward all children in our class, we have to allow them to develop their own interests and use their distinctive learning styles. Sleeter (2005) maintains that standards and standardization are not the same thing (p. 3).

> Allowing for development of diversity in expertise can serve as an intellectual resource for constructive participation in a multicultural democracy and diverse world. It is to our benefit that we *not* all learn the same thing, beyond the basic skills.
>
> (p. 7)

Applying this to curriculum planning, Sleeter says:

> It is the teacher's responsibility to find out, become familiar with, and respect the knowledge students bring to school, and to organize curriculum and learning activities in such a way that students are able to activate and use that knowledge.
>
> (p. 106)

Similarly, Moll and Gonzalez (2004) stress the importance of utilizing the "fund of knowledge" each student brings to the classroom.

Among our study participants, Nina said that

> when you teach a lesson you have to think about every child, you can't just teach in one way; for example, you have to ask yourself whether

this child is going to understand the language, or whether that child has to move around a lot.

Another new teacher reported that in trying to make the topic of "medieval times" meaningful for her students, she often departs from traditional content to a degree, giving illustrations from the medieval history of the non-European cultures represented in her class. Many saw giving one-on-one attention to academically less successful students as quite effective. Vera observed that "some students in my class function much better with a one-on-one situation, while others do just fine in the larger group. So you have to look at the individual child." Anna spoke of the need to identify gaps in students' background knowledge and give them as much exposure as possible to information and experiences in these areas; or alternatively, to find books that are more suited to their distinctive background, e.g., urban settings.

ELL students (English Language Learners) are a particular subgroup who increase the complexity of individualizing the curriculum. Many of the new teachers described how they attempt to help these students, usually without special training. Speaking of the need to support ELL students, Felicity said: "It's just social justice, really . . . all these children should be given opportunities." She described one activity she developed to help her ELL students learn while also promoting their interaction with the rest of the class:

> One thing I've implemented to help them is a dictionary game. Two of the ELL students will tell the class the first letter of a word they are looking at and read the definition, and the class has to guess the word. It's great fun, they love it . . . and I'm sure it benefits them, because a lot of what they don't understand is vocabulary.

Sophia tries to include her ELL students in the class as much as possible, and finds that applying a "multiple intelligences" approach (Gardner, 1999) benefits them along with the other students. At the end of her second year she said that the progress of her ELL students that year had been remarkable "because there is so much opportunity for them to use their language and socialize with others. Also, because they have such a language-rich environment – with visuals and activities that revolve around language – they quickly start to associate sound, meaning, and word."

Study diverse cultures

Studying different cultures – their distinctive ideas, customs, and achievements – is of course a major aspect of inclusive education. It is essential both to increase respect for people who come from these cultures and to aid interaction between different societal groups. It also gives a basis for seeing similarities and differences among groups. Many of the new teachers emphasized that study of various cultures is an important foundation for mutual understanding and respect in the classroom. Felicity commented:

> We did a lot of diversity studies [in the pre-service program] and although I haven't done enough of it this year, because it's been too hectic, I really want to be the kind of teacher who perceives literature that's not mainstream, that's diverse . . . It's really important that the students see themselves reflected in the literature, or see other cultures reflected in it, not just the mainstream one.

Maria reported:

> One of my girls found a book on Islam and she said, "This is my religion, Miss G"; and I said, "I know, go ahead and read it." So I try to select books that reflect the diversity in the class, and we talk about it, mainly during literacy.

Anita observed:

> This class likes [to learn] about different cultures, they're very interested in Chinese culture, African culture, and so on, so I bring those things in. For example, at Christmas time we talked a lot about Kwanzaa, and although nobody in the class celebrates Kwanzaa we talked about it anyway. Actually . . . holiday time in December is a nice time to talk a lot about the festivals of different cultures, and the students really like it.

Support students in developing their individual way of life

Besides studying the heritage cultures in the community, we should also help students develop their *individual* way of life, against the background of their culture and community. Teachers need to initiate discussion of how individual way of life development can clash with traditional cultural beliefs and practices. Although teachers certainly need to respect and build on the culture of the home and local community, they must also respect the wishes of individual students. Carrie spoke of the problem of "parents who have issues of their own and don't seem to have good boundaries" in relation to their children.

Students vary greatly in how much they wish to adhere to their heritage culture (and often they belong to several). Teachers need to be aware of this and talk with the students about conflicts that may arise between cultural imperatives and individual needs and how these conflicts might be addressed. Sometimes poststructuralists and other theorists have over-emphasized sociocultural factors in human life, not acknowledging sufficiently the permeability and fluidity of identities and ways of life and the "third spaces" that can be created (LeCourt, 2004; New London Group, 1996; Pahl and Rowsell, 2005). Home and local cultures, just like dominant ones, can be authoritarian and limiting in certain respects. In this regard, Barton and Hamilton (1998) comment:

> [I]t is important to stress that vernacular literacies are still subject to social pressures of the family and other social groups and they are regulated by them. While these pressures may be less formal than the strictures of the school, law, or work-place, and people may often willingly accept them, institutions such as the family are powerful social institutions, and their influence can be strongly restraining to people.
>
> (p. 253)

Accordingly, teachers must help their students to *both* understand, value, and draw on their home and local culture(s) *and* develop an identity and way of life distinctly their own.

The importance of connecting to students' everyday life was a recurring theme in the new teacher interviews. Candice gave as her "philosophy on literacy learning" that students should "be encouraged from where they are; it should be exciting, and they should see how it matters in their day to day life." Anita recalled learning in her pre-service program "the theory of how to facilitate kids talking about books and figuring out the parts they enjoyed and making the experience enjoyable for them." She also said:

> If it doesn't have meaning, what's the point? If it doesn't have meaning for them, they're not going to be engaged and be excited by reading and writing. So I guess my aim is to try to make things as meaningful to them as possible, connecting reading to writing, connecting to the things they read personally, relating things to the real world, their interests, and their lives. Because at this age . . . if things are too abstract they tend not to be engaged and then they're not actually learning anything.

Discuss issues of prejudice and discrimination explicitly

Although we believe inclusive education should largely be "infused" into the life of the classroom, the teacher–student relationship, the study of diverse cultures, and so on, there is definitely a place for explicit, critical discussion of issues of inclusion. Even in elementary school, students should begin to learn about the history and mechanisms of prejudice and discrimination.

They should come to understand how ideology pervades popular culture, how formal knowledge is molded by the interests of dominant groups, and how "the other" is distorted, suppressed, and often just ignored by popular culture and academic disciplines. And they should learn how even minority groups themselves often internalize ideology-based beliefs about them (Freire, 1968/72). Raising these issues might appear to open the way to a strident, authoritarian approach to inclusion that undermines constructivist teaching and an interactive teacher–student relationship, but we believe that with care this can be avoided. The topics can be addressed in a sensitive, dialogical manner within a supportive class community. Where individual students become angry or defensive when the issues are raised, the very approach to human relationships being advocated can be modeled in the way these reactions are dealt with.

Many of the new teachers in our study saw the importance of explicit discussion in this area. Nina reported that she talks about racial and cultural diversity with her students and, in particular, the inappropriateness of linking race and national identity. Paul spoke of the need for explicit attention to problems of stereotyping, including self-stereotyping:

> In my school a lot of teachers focus on citizenship, values, and that kind of thing . . . because there are a number of students whose main barrier to any kind of learning is their attitude, the way they interact, their approach. For instance, there are boys who feel that being smart is not for boys, it's a girl thing. So reading books, oh well, you shouldn't do that if you're a guy because it's not cool. And the few boys in my class who are good readers are quiet about it and a bit hesitant; and it's the same with a couple of good writers . . . And I think you have to teach them that people should do what they're good at, they should work on that.

Anna uses examples and analogies to help her students understand that people who have different views from us or come from different cultures and religions are often "different, not bad." Wanda said:

> We talk a lot about people of different backgrounds and cultures and how we are all the same, we're all people, we all have skin, we all breathe the same air. And when we look at the different holidays and celebrations, we discuss how we must honor all of them.

Recommendations for pre-service education

Based on the views and practices of the new teachers in our study, relevant literature in the field, and our own experience and reflections, we make the following recommendations for addressing inclusion in pre-service education.

Adopt an infusion approach

To begin, we wish to advocate infusion of an inclusive approach throughout the pre-service program, including the cohort community and the field experiences. This is in keeping with the new teachers' preference for infusion and the arguments of some key writers in the area. Although there is a place for special classes, workshops, and courses on inclusive education, the bulk of the work on this topic should be integrated into other aspects of the program (Darling-Hammond, 2002; Irvine, 2003; Vavrus, 2002). If inclusion is mainly discussed separately from the rest of the program, it tends to be seen as tokenism or an "add-on" by student teachers and not taken seriously; also, its theoretical significance and implications for practice may not actually be understood (Villegas and Lucas, 2002).

Avoid stereotyping

As discussed before, rather than dwelling too much on the differences between various racial, ethnic, gender, and other categories, we favor a balanced study of both differences and commonalities. This is important in order to avoid stereotyping, which is itself a major form of prejudice (Irvine, 2003; Melnick and Zeichner, 1997). This does not mean that all individuals and groups are the same: on the contrary, there are often significant differences in interests, tastes, temperament, and so on. However, student teachers need to realize that the diversity within groups is much greater than that between them, and that people from different groups have a great many commonalities (Darling-Hammond, 2002; Irvine, 2003). The vast majority of human differences simply do not run along racial, ethnic, gender, age, class, or other sub-category lines.

Use a constructivist approach

Although there should be explicit advocacy and discussion of inclusive education, and infusion of such an approach throughout the program, ultimately student teachers must take ownership of their development in this domain. This is essential if our treatment of the topic is to be dialogical and constructivist in nature rather than top-down. A transmission pedagogy regarding inclusion, as with any other area, stifles motivation and intelligent pursuit of goals. Our efforts should be directed toward ensuring that inclusion becomes something that appeals to student teachers, interests them, and makes sense to them, something they commit themselves to and implement largely under their own steam. Otherwise they will quickly abandon it when exposed to the rigors of the practicum and their first years of teaching. This is a difficult stance for teacher educators to take, especially in the area of inclusion where injustices abound and the stakes are so high for pupil well-being. However, short-cut authoritarian methods are less effective in both the short and the long run (Schoonmaker, 2002; Vavrus, 2002); and besides, if we use them in this area, we undercut our general advocacy of a constructivist approach to teaching.

Model class community and a close teacher–student relationship

Class community should not only be discussed with student teachers but modeled in the program (Darling-Hammond, 2002; Irvine, 2003; Vavrus, 2002). Modeling an inclusive community takes the pre-service program beyond lectures, reading, and discussion and allows students to see first-hand what is involved in running an inclusive classroom. An inclusive pre-service community also gives student teachers an experience of inclusive living and the opportunity to learn what "others" are like: that they are human beings like themselves and often "kindred spirits."

Apart from experiencing community with their peers, student teachers need a relatively close relationship with faculty if they are to explore and adopt an inclusive approach to teaching. They need a connection with faculty who clearly believe in an inclusive approach and who show by their words and actions that they will back them up in developing this approach, both on the university campus and in the practicum. They also need to see for themselves how important the teacher–student relationship is in fostering inclusion in the classroom, and come to understand how to build such relationships with their own students.

Go deeply into issues of inclusion and exclusion

Although modeling and a constructivist approach are important in this area, there is also a need for deep, critical study of issues of inclusion. Student teachers have to understand clearly the reasons for inclusion and the harm that is done by its opposite. Furthermore, faculty must feel free to state explicitly their own views about inclusion and equity. Sometimes it is suggested that instructors should keep their opinions to themselves – *especially* in moral and cultural areas – in order to avoid indoctrination. But we believe that, on the contrary, indoctrination is more likely to occur if instructors try to hide their views, since students quickly figure out what their views are but lack the opportunity to critique them in an open, systematic manner. Indoctrination is avoided not by refraining from expressing our opinions but rather by creating a setting in which students have time – and encouragement – to discuss, disagree, propose alternatives, and ultimately develop their own point of view.

Establish appropriate field experiences

Providing relevant field experiences during the program can expose student teachers to types of diversity, prejudice, and disadvantage not encountered before. It can also give them the opportunity to build on their prior experiences and modify their ideas and practices in this area. We have already discussed the role of the cohort community experience in fostering an inclusive approach to teaching. Two other sets of experiences frequently mentioned in the literature are those occurring in the practicum (Darling-Hammond, 2002) and in the world beyond the school (Cochran-Smith, Davis, and Fries, 2004; Irvine, 2003; Villegas and Lucas, 2002). In order to hone their philosophy of inclusion and their skills in this area, student teachers need practicum placements in schools with a diverse student body. Direct experience of communities beyond the school is also widely advocated as a way of enabling student teachers to learn about diversity and inclusion.

Conclusion

In the past, the term "inclusive education" has been used in a rather narrow sense to refer to the mainstreaming of "special education" students in regular classrooms. In line with growing practice, we use the term here much more broadly to refer to teaching that not only accommodates academic difference but is sensitive to differences of gender, class, race, ethnicity, language, physical ability, and so on. Such teaching is necessary (a) to optimize the learning of all pupils, whatever their abilities, interests, and background, and (b) to help pupils understand the nature of prejudice and discrimination and acquire inclusive attitudes and behaviors.

Clearly, inclusive education should be a high priority in pre-service preparation. It is not just a frill or political nicety; it is fundamental to a progressive, constructivist pedagogy that strives to meet the needs and build on the experiences of all students. It is inherent in the respectful, dia-logical, individualized approach to teaching we have discussed so far in this book. However, attention must be given to the *manner* in which inclusive education is promoted in pre-service education. Rather than imposing it top-down, we should embody inclusive education in the program, model it ourselves, and use dialogical methods to encourage student teachers to take personal ownership of an inclusive approach.

Chapter 5

Subject content and pedagogy

In recent decades, teacher education has tended to focus on theory and "general method," to the relative neglect of content and pedagogy specific to subjects such as literacy, math, and science. For example, it is not uncommon to find elementary pre-service programs with just one 40-hour course on literacy teaching and even less on math or science. In our view, it is time to return to giving higher priority to subject specific knowledge in pre-service preparation. Although teacher educators were right to reject the earlier assumption (still widespread in the public at large) that subject knowledge is *all* one needs in order to teach well, we have often gone too far to the other extreme. Much of the school day is spent teaching specific subjects and accordingly teachers must be prepared for this work.

To illustrate the kind of subject specific knowledge new teachers need we begin with a profile of Wanda, a participant in our study who was exceptional in her knowledge of content and pedagogy in the area of literacy; as we will see, much of her knowledge was gained outside her pre-service program.

Wanda

> My philosophy [of literacy teaching] is making sure that I have a literacy-rich classroom environment and that I'm giving these children every opportunity to be exposed to literacy. Whether it's the books they take home, the information here in the classroom, or even just the dialogue about reading, I am trying to teach them that reading is good, literacy is good, and it's fun.

Background

Wanda came to teaching as a second career, having spent 16 years in the financial sector managing pension funds. Her undergraduate degree was in economics and political science and she completed an MBA in finance. She is a mother of three, has traveled extensively, and has lived abroad.

After her years in business, where she achieved considerable success, she returned to university and gained her teaching credential specializing in kindergarten through grade 6. Although she has been actively involved in her own children's schooling, she noted in her third year of teaching that "teaching is definitely a much tougher job than I ever imagined it to be." Since being certified, she has taught in two different urban schools, initially teaching a combined grade 1/2 class and then grade 2/3 classes in her second and third years. Because of lack of openings, she has yet to be granted a "regular" contract by the school district and so has no job security.

Not surprisingly, given her initial career path, Wanda's undergraduate and previous graduate degrees were not related to teaching young children, but she felt her work in the business world helped her because "you learn how to talk to people, you learn how to have empathy, and that's the key." Her experience in pension fund management was one of the reasons she decided to drastically change her professional life and go into teaching. When working with clients, she realized that many people who had to make decisions about their own pensions had only functional literacy, which led her to conclude that there is "something wrong with the education system."

At first Wanda was not enthusiastic about her teacher education program, but as time went on she identified aspects that had influenced her. Her two literacy instructors she described as "incredible." She noted that "they took almost every opportunity to show how a book could be used to introduce a topic or drive a lesson." They introduced the students to publishers and a range of resources. She also completed the optional training in Tribes, which she found very helpful, and she continues to use many community-building strategies learned in the pre-service program. Her two practice teaching placements – in grades 3 and 6 – did not seem to her to be particularly strong. The former was a very structured program and the latter she thought actually inhibited learning. Nevertheless, she felt "practice teaching was extremely useful, just because it puts you in a real-life situation."

Description of practice

Wanda does not approach literacy as a series of subjects (e.g. spelling, writing, grammar); rather, her entire program has literacy at the core. She has reading and writing workshops; reading is often the springboard for writing; she aims to build self-esteem in her students as readers and writers; there are extended periods for reading and writing every day; she integrates literacy into other subject areas (e.g., *A Clock for a Dreamer* to introduce a geometry unit); students learn developmentally appropriate strategies for reading and writing (e.g., picture clues for emergent readers); students can respond to texts in many different ways (e.g., through visual arts); children are invited to talk about their learning and their preferred learning style;

students participate in literature circles; and students have considerable choice in reading materials and writing topics and activities.

The range of materials in Wanda's classroom is extensive – leveled books, high-quality children's books, non-fiction texts, multiple copies of the same book, books at different reading levels, books on tape, books by the same author – all beautifully displayed, accessible to the children, and well used. Central to Wanda's practice are her literacy centers. The children work often at the centers (making words, listening, writing, doing guided reading) and she changes the centers regularly. Being a parent, she understands the importance of the school-home connection and finds ways to involve parents. She has established a Borrow-a-Book program and, recognizing that many parents do not speak English (but have home computers), she encourages them to use CD-ROMs with their children because they have pictures and voice-over.

Wanda aims to get to know each child individually, discovering his or her interests and strengths.

> The reality is that everybody learns at their own pace. In order to have a successful program, you have to insure there is solid grounding in the basic principles of literacy. And in order for a child to be successful, they have to like what they're doing. As a teacher, I have to try not so much to teach a child as to create an environment that makes it so enjoyable the child will want to read, learn, and continue to question and grow. And that is very individual. Different children have different needs and interests. So [I have] to be able to [develop] a program that's going to appeal to more than just one style of learner: not just one type of literature, it has to be a mixture of everything.

She uses a variety of class configurations – whole-class, small-group, and individual – matching them to the goals of the lesson. Her groups are fluid, sometimes heterogeneous and sometimes formed according to ability.

Wanda is required to use the DRA reading assessment system but she supplements it with her own data gathering in order to find out more about the children. "Assessment is not just black and white. There's going to be a lot of grey." She observes the children, listens to them read, holds individual writing conferences, talks to them about their learning, and sets clear goals for each unit that she shares with the children. Wanda does not want to simply assign a mark; rather, she wants to understand what the child has actually learned.

Sources of learning

We were particularly interested to find out how Wanda had acquired such deep knowledge of literacy and literacy teaching, given that her preservice program included only one course in this area. With her business background, there was not an obvious prior link with literacy. In some of the interviews we included questions specifically on sources of professional learning.

Own experience as a reader and writer

Wanda emphasized that she is a reader and writer. "I love books, I love reading. And that was something that was always very strong within my own upbringing and about who I am as a person. My husband and I both love reading, so that's there." Valuing reading and writing in her personal life and understanding herself as a reader and writer were the foundations for her development as a literacy teacher.

Influence of family

Wanda's family played a key role in the teacher she became. Teaching was part of her mother's family tradition.

> My mother was a teacher for five decades and she was my mentor in this respect. If I could, I would model myself after her. Up until she died, she constantly had either former students or their parents coming up to her and basically thanking her for what they gained from her. She ended her career in Special Education; she always used to say that every child can learn, they just need to be given the time and the approach to learn.

When Wanda secured her first teaching position, she turned to her family for help, in particular a cousin who was a retired curriculum consultant.

> She came in a couple of weeks before school, we set up the classroom, she had a substantial number of resources. She also had a friend, a primary years consultant who had just retired, and I got a lot of her resources as well. We laid out a plan of attack for my first month or two.

Working with her own children provided first-hand experience with literacy. Her two daughters were always keen readers but her youngest child – her son – was a reluctant reader who would rather have played video games than read a book. Enticing him into reading helped her learn strategies for engaging children in her class.

Influence of a model school

Wanda's first teaching position was in what was deemed a model literacy school. The principal was a true curriculum leader and the in-school Literacy Coordinator became Wanda's informal mentor. The school engaged in school-wide literacy initiatives. For example, February was poetry month, which meant that the whole school focused on poetry, poets visited the school to talk about being poets and writing poetry, staff attended workshops on writing poetry, and the school celebrated the children's poems. When the entire faculty adopted Lucy Calkins' approach to writing, teachers in division teams decided what forms of writing they would focus on. Teachers worked in grade teams to develop common curriculum expectations, review their approach to assessment, and plan teaching activities. Although each teacher was allowed flexibility in the strategies used, there was a consistent philosophy of literacy learning throughout the school. The principal provided many outside learning opportunities as well; for example, the school was chosen as one of 17 schools to visit New York City to observe exemplary literacy programs. Fortunately, Wanda's own views of reading and writing resonated with the philosophy advocated in this school, and this allowed her to advance her knowledge of literacy curriculum, pedagogy, and assessment. She spoke very highly of the experience and regretted having to leave the school.

Professional learning

Wanda truly took control of her learning and capitalized on everything that was offered. Before entering the teacher education program, she volunteered for over 200 hours in a primary teacher's classroom. The teacher, who had been a cooperating teacher for many years with the OISE/UT preservice program, had an outstanding literacy program, and was a strong mentor. Wanda spent substantial time reading professional literature. On her own initiative she read Debbie Miller, Sharon Taberski, Lucy Calkins, Irene Fountas, Gay Su Pinnell, and Patricia Cunningham. She acquired an extensive collection of teacher resource books, often spending her own money to purchase them. When she left her first school she remained on the listserv of the Literacy Coordinator, which allowed her to access the school district internal literacy website. She identified a grade 3 teacher in the district who had a website where he described his literacy centers. "I've been looking through his website as fast as I can to get ideas." Wanda enrolled in summer workshops in areas where she felt she needed to strengthen her program (e.g., science and art). She also completed an in-service course on special education.

Wanda's class in action

Entering Wanda's combined grade 2/3 class was enchanting. The classroom was old but bright. Books were everywhere but well organized, children's work was on display, charts were hung across the room, motivational posters decorated the walls, one of the reading centers had stuffed animals, and desks were organized in groups. Although the group of children Wanda taught in her third year were particularly challenging, she truly cared for each student and worked patiently with all.

When students entered the class, they immediately focused on organizing their agenda, homework, money for the pizza lunch, and so on. Once this "housekeeping" was done, students began to read silently. Some wandered over to the literacy corner and curled up with a stuffed animal, some read in pairs, others stayed at their desks. Most were engrossed in their reading. After about 20 minutes of reading, Wanda gathered the students to continue working on their novel. They reviewed the events from *Stone Fox* before she began to read aloud; during and after the reading they discussed the events. Wanda's questions probed the motives of the characters and the impact of events on them. As a follow-up writing activity, students had to write a journal entry from the perspective of one of the characters, describing how he or she was feeling about the events that had just occurred. For about 20 minutes students worked on their writing, obviously comfortable with the task, using invented spelling and sharing their work with each other. When they reconvened on the carpet some students read their work aloud, with Wanda commenting on the strengths of each piece.

After recess, the class had a science lesson. They had been studying soil and started the lesson with a review of why some of the class plants had flourished and others had not. Wanda then formed random groups for a game of Jeopardy focused on soil. The students had previously written questions and answers for the game. There was lots of laughter and enthusiasm for the game. The students understood the concepts, having recently completed a project on an animal that lives underground. Wanda had read them *Diary of a Worm*, and they had to research an animal or insect of their choice that lives in the soil and do a diary entry for it.

Final thoughts

Wanda is an interesting case because she has acquired a great deal of knowledge outside her teacher education program. At the heart of Wanda is an insatiable desire to learn; whether she is in the business world or in education, she is a learner. Admittedly she is unusual in that she seems to have an innate understanding of reading and writing processes. However, she has not simply relied on her natural talent: she spends countless hours learning both theory and practical strategies. Actually, we worry that Wanda is setting the bar too high. In our interviews, she talked about the substantial time she devotes to planning her program (e.g., acquiring suitable texts and searching the internet for lessons or resources). In her first year of teaching, she often spent most of Saturday and Sunday planning lessons and units, and we are not sure her planning time has decreased substantially since then. But if in the future Wanda has to ease up a bit, in the interests of personal well-being, it is clear she will continue to learn and be an outstanding teacher.

The influence of the model literacy school in Wanda's first year shows the potential of immersing a novice teacher in such a setting. She had many opportunities to learn, was able to observe good practice, and had support in building her program.

> The staff worked as a community, I was exposed to so much. It was just the wealth of knowledge they had. Their approach was very holistic in terms of looking at a child and trying to figure out how to approach the learning for him or her.

Such an experience would be ideal for all beginning teachers and in turn would have enormous benefit for pupils.

What and why of subject content and pedagogy

Wanda's profile illustrates the kind of subject-specific knowledge we believe should be given high priority in teacher preparation. Through extensive life experiences, mentoring, and pre-service and in-service education, Wanda attained both (a) relevant knowledge of literacy and (b) knowledge of literacy pedagogy. These two knowledges overlap, of course, because the first is that content knowledge needed to *teach* the subject, not just the knowledge "generally acquired by individuals who pursue a college major in a content field" (Grossman and Schoenfeld, 2005, pp. 206–207). The combination of knowledge of types (a) and (b) is often referred to as "pedagogical content knowledge" (Shulman, 1986; Shulman, 2004), a term that explicitly brings together content and pedagogy.

(a) The *content* component of subject knowledge is "the aspects of content most germane to its teachability" (Shulman, 2004, p. 203). In literacy, for example, the content knowledge teachers need includes:

- knowledge of genres (e.g., non-fiction, realistic fiction, fairy tales, drama, poetry, graphic novels, film, e-mail correspondence, weblogs, text messages)
- personal experience, enjoyment, and appreciation of various genres
- knowledge of specific works of adult literature, children's literature, and young adult literature
- knowledge of why people read and write
- knowledge of the processes used in reading (e.g., drawing on phonemic awareness, activating prior substantive and vocabulary knowledge) and writing (e.g., having a sense of audience, finding one's voice as a writer).

(b) The subject-specific *pedagogical* knowledge teachers need includes:

- knowledge of "ways of representing and formulating the subject" that are especially powerful in deepening pupils' understanding and appreciation of it (Shulman, 2004, p. 203)

- awareness of which genres, works, topics, and themes within the subject are of most interest to pupils
- familiarity with the typical blocks and misunderstandings pupils experience in relation to the subject – "what kinds of errors or mistakes students are likely to make" (Grossman and Schoenfeld, 2005, p. 205)
- knowledge of especially effective activities for teaching the subject in the classroom
- knowledge of child development and relevant cultural backgrounds in relation to the subject: for example, the typical "learning progressions" (Shepard, Hammerness, Darling-Hammond, and Rust, 2005, p. 280) of children and "the conceptions and preconceptions that students of different ages and backgrounds bring with them to the learning" (Shulman, 2004, p. 203)
- knowledge of available textbooks, published programs, and other learning materials in the subject (Shulman, 2004, pp. 203–204).

Why is subject knowledge (content and pedagogy) important for teaching? On the one hand, teachers need to know a subject themselves in order to teach it well. If they are to engage students and teach in depth, teachers must be able to choose from a wealth of content they understand and appreciate. As Hagger and McIntyre (2006) say:

> Clearly teachers . . . need a thorough and rich knowledge of the subject matter that they are teaching. Unless teachers feel secure about what they are teaching, they tend to teach in a defensive way, sticking to a set, pre-planned script, concentrating on communicating what they know and avoiding as much as possible thoughtful questions from pupils.
>
> (p. 5)

Further, to individualize instruction teachers have to be able to find examples and explanations – often on the spur of the moment – appropriate to particular students. According to Ball (2000):

> [U]nderstanding subject matter is essential to listening flexibly to others and hearing what they are saying or where they might be heading. Knowing content is also crucial to being inventive in creating worthwhile opportunities for learning that take learners' experiences, interests, and needs into account.
>
> (p. 242)

Finally, integrating a subject with other subjects "across the curriculum" – an essential aspect of sound teaching – requires knowing in detail its connections with other subjects.

Turning to subject-specific *pedagogical* knowledge, this too is necessary if one is to teach effectively. Student teachers will not understand the general pedagogy we advocate in pre-service programs unless we illustrate it in the context of particular subjects. Many of the new teachers in our study had difficulty applying to their literacy teaching the principles and strategies learned in pre-service, such as collaborative learning, student construction of knowledge, and classroom assessment. Anita, as we saw earlier, wanted pre-service instructors to give more practical examples: "This worked for me, here is one thing you can do, or a variety of things . . . you can start with these and then see what works for you."

Because the time available for the professional aspect of the program is short, teacher educators are tempted to focus mainly on general pedagogy and "leave to individual teachers the challenge of integrating subject matter knowledge and pedagogy in the context of their work" (Ball, 2000, p. 242). However, according to Ball, although we assume that such integration "is simple and happens in the course of experience," in fact it "does not happen easily, and often does not happen at all" (p. 242). With respect to assessment, for example, Shepard et al. (2005) maintain that pre-service instruction must be largely subject-specific. In their discussion of assessment, the authors begin with a focus on content because "assessment is meaningless if it does not engage those things that we most want students to learn" (p. 280). These authors also stress the need to make the learning of child development subject-specific: "Beginning elementary teachers should be familiar with the learning progressions in early literacy and mathematics development and be able to plan instructional and intervention strategies that help students take the next steps" (p. 284).

Problems of subject content and pedagogy

Although the need is clear, there are many challenges to ensuring that new teachers have sufficient knowledge of subject content and pedagogy when they enter the profession. The most obvious one is the lack of time in the typical pre-service program for subject-specific courses. This is especially glaring at the elementary level, where a teacher may be responsible for half a dozen subjects or more. There are constant pleas to increase the length of pre-service programs, but in most cases neither governments nor those who wish to be teachers feel they can afford the additional costs involved; accordingly, the overall time available is likely to stay much the same.

The pre-service programs from which the teachers in our study came did have courses (though not many) on teaching specific subjects. But another challenge in teacher preparation is knowing what balance to strike *within* such courses between general and specific matters. Subject instructors often place greater emphasis on general issues than on specific content and pedagogy: for example, a literacy instructor may discuss multiple intelligences, community building, activity methods, group work, action research, and constructivist learning. In our view, although subject instructors should address general pedagogical theory and principles, they should normally do so specifically in relation to their subject, constantly illustrating the general in terms of the particular.

A further difficulty is that even if student teachers have studied one or more relevant disciplines at the undergraduate level, they have often not done so in the *manner* needed for subject teaching. Their knowledge may be too specialized or technical, having been acquired for different purposes from those that apply in the school setting. They may not have explored the links between subjects as required for teaching across the curriculum. And they may not have given much attention to connections to everyday life. Goodlad (1966) long ago drew attention to the pitfalls of simply basing the school curriculum on "the structure of disciplines," without regard for relevance or student interest.

Even more problematic, of course, is the situation where student teachers have little or no undergraduate background in their teaching subjects. Although this is more likely to occur at the elementary level, many high school teachers will also have to teach "out of field" at some stage in their career. Pre-service programs often attempt to overcome this problem by making relevant subject background a condition of admission to the program, or requiring students to take relevant arts and science courses during the program; and we believe more needs to be done along these lines. However, such measures are often not very successful, partly because of lack of applicants in key subject areas, and partly owing to shortage of suitable undergraduate arts and science courses. Moreover, we face a dilemma when applicants apparently have considerable potential as teachers but limited knowledge in relevant subjects: should we reject them in favor of others who have more subject knowledge but otherwise seem less suited to teaching?

Finally, apart from lack of subject background among student teachers, we pre-service faculty can also be somewhat patchy in subject content and pedagogy. We too are frequently expected to teach out of field, at least to a degree. Because of the inadequate resources usually allocated to teacher education in colleges and universities, it is often not possible to hire the subject instructors needed. One may argue that it is best to hire faculty with a sound general approach to teaching and teacher education and then have them adapt to subject instruction on the job. But it can take many years for such instructors to acquire sufficient subject-specific knowledge, especially given the typically heavy faculty workload in pre-service education and the lack of provision for professional development for pre-service faculty.

Principles and strategies of subject content and pedagogy

It is apparent, then, that the challenges of ensuring adequate knowledge of subject content and pedagogy among teachers are many. However, we believe progress can be made if we have a clear understanding of what is needed. In this section, we focus on ways to approach subject-specific knowledge in the school context; in the next, we look at implications for teacher education. As in other chapters, we draw on both the research literature and our own study of new teachers.

Select relevant, interesting subject content and activities

The first point to recognize is that not all content is of equal relevance and interest. Teachers must select carefully, and enlist the help of pupils in the selection. As we saw in Chapter 1, teachers often have considerable control over what is emphasized in a given subject area. We should use this control to make subject learning as worthwhile to pupils as possible. Apart from carefully selecting content for the whole class, we should help individual students find topics and activities that are engaging and important to them. Atwell (1998) describes how she went from giving her grade 8 students very little say in reading materials to allowing them to choose (with some negotiation) virtually all the books they read (pp. 31–35). Although this sometimes resulted in their choosing an inappropriate book, it meant that "they averaged thirty-five titles [a year], from Blume to Bronte, Voigt to Verne" (p. 34), and the classroom discussions based on all this reading were energetic and rich.

Darling-Hammond et al. (2005) give examples of "decisions and adaptations" with regard to subject content and activities (p. 175). They note that, in mathematics, one teacher may spend "only thirty minutes explaining nonlinear functions" whereas another may devote weeks to the same topic in a course "by the same name, even using the same textbook" (pp. 181–182). They also describe the differences between two English classes, both studying Sophocles' *Oedipus the King*:

> In one group, the teacher assigns the reading of the book as homework, holds two days of discussion about the book in class, and has students take a test on the book emphasizing new vocabulary and facts about characters and plot details. In the other group, the teacher provides a choice of essay questions, such as "Was Oedipus a victim of fate or did he create his own destiny?", a month in advance. She begins the unit with a contemporary essay about the *Oedipus complex*, relating this common term to what students are about to read. They read the book over two weeks, combining daily read-alouds and dramatic

presentations of the play with nightly reading for homework and guided journal questions . . . [The teacher reads their journals and gives feedback.] . . . Class discussions in large and small groups take up these questions and probe them further. The class also stages a debate on the question of Oedipus' responsibility for his fate; students then write a series of drafts regarding the essay question chosen, with peer review and teacher review before completing a major essay on the book.

(p. 182)

Develop broad goals and principles for content selection

As we select interesting subject content for students – involving them in the process – we should do so with purpose: it should never be *just* to keep them interested and active. As discussed in Chapter 1, we must constantly ask, "What are they likely to learn from this content?" Often instead of giving students completely free rein we should negotiate topics and learning materials with them. In Atwell's (1998) approach to readers workshop, mentioned above, she often discusses various possibilities with her students. This requires that she "read and skim a lot of books and consider their merits and [her] own criteria, as a teacher of literature and of adolescents" (p. 38).

Further, we should not just focus on what is *currently* interesting and relevant to students. A large part of students' reality is needing to do well in the school system in the future and gain the knowledge and skills required to enter post-secondary levels and ultimately find suitable employment. Many students are aware of this and become impatient when teachers place too much emphasis on "life learning" and moment-by-moment engagement. However, as far as possible we should combine studying what they "have to know" with exploring matters that are both intrinsically interesting and relevant to broader life goals.

We must, then, be fairly directed in our subject teaching, focusing on key knowledge and skills. Along these lines, Anita said we should ask: "Okay . . . what are the main skills students need to know in, say, the context of science that will take them forward in their learning?" Felicity reported: "Previously I tended to be eclectic – teaching interesting bits and pieces here and there – or perhaps chaotic might be a better word. But now [year 3] I'm becoming more coherent, which is exciting: I think my teaching will improve with that approach." Similarly, Jeannie observed:

I think literacy teaching should be explicit and directed: you go in with a goal and the kids have an opportunity to learn in a particular area and then practice it. For example, with "making connections" . . . I explicitly teach the skills, whether through modeling, discussion, read-alouds; then they have a lot of opportunity to practice the skills on their own; and then they come back as a group and share and debrief.

Integrate subject teaching

Teaching literacy, math, technology, etc. "across the curriculum" is widely recommended today. For one thing, it can connect subject study more closely to the real world: in everyday life, topics do not come in separate disciplines (Wood, 1992). Moreover, cross-curricular study can increase the depth of learning. For example, the general principle of being critical can be taught, illustrated, and applied in relation to both scientific theories and literary works, thus deepening students' understanding of the principle as well as the subjects. However, we must ensure that we take the extra step of illustrating and applying principles *in specific subjects*. Not only will students frequently fail to apply a general principle to new areas on their own, but principles often have different meanings in different subjects. Darling-Hammond et al. (2005) note that although infusion of computer technology across the curriculum is appropriate, students should be helped to see that computer "visualization" may be used differently in chemistry from in biology, and the use of "database tools" is rather distinctive in the social sciences (p. 199).

Many of the participants in our study stressed the importance of integrating subjects. For example, Anita said: "I wanted the students to learn report writing – which Calkins doesn't cover – and to integrate social studies into my language program, so I made up my own unit for that, with a lot of use of computers." Marisa took an exceptionally strong stand on the need for interdisciplinary study, although she was also clearly in favor of teaching individual subjects well.

> I don't think it matters whether [an elementary teacher] is a specialist or not . . . I can learn [the content] and apply it in my class . . . My fear is that if you have specialists they will teach using lectures and so on, and integration with other curriculum areas will be more difficult. This applies especially to kindergarten through grade 6; but I know some middle schools that are moving away from rotary because they're realizing that chunking the subjects is not effective.

Collaborate with other teachers in subject teaching

Working with colleagues in teaching content can increase integration, help with lesson preparation, and make teaching more enjoyable. It can also model a collaborative approach to inquiry. As we saw in Chapter 1, by their third year many of the participants in our study were using the same learning programs as their colleagues, while modifying them in certain ways. Vera described how, at her school,

> the grade 1 team sits down every week, and we bring our materials, what we've done in the past, what we've seen done, and our research on other programs. We decide what our focus will be and what we want to do; and then we copy and distribute it.

As far as possible, collaboration in teaching subjects should occur not only in a grade or division but throughout the school. In this way, students can get used to certain terms and methods; key concepts, principles, and skills can be taught in depth; and unnecessary repetition can be avoided. Felicity said that she and her colleagues "try to work as a team within the school in literacy"; for example, "at the beginning of the year we had a school initiative on letter writing . . . and we're hoping to do more of that, so everyone's on the same page in what we're teaching and next year we'll know what the students have done and can build on that." Marisa commented:

> I think [collaboration] is extremely important, both within a division or grade but also school-wide. All teachers need to be speaking the same language (although of course you would modify that according to the students' level of understanding). For example, if you're teaching the elements of a story, everyone would call the events "events," or you might call it "plot": but it would be consistent right from kindergarten to grade 5 so it wouldn't confuse the kids. Also the types of resources would be the same, and . . . even the type of graphic organizers we use should be consistent . . . so the kids know exactly what to do. Having said that, we should know what writing forms are being taught in each grade so we don't repeat certain things and miss out on others: there needs to be a cohesiveness in literacy teaching in the school.

As a teacher, pursue subject matter knowledge and appreciation yourself

In order to teach our subjects well, we *teachers* must continue to grow in knowledge and appreciation of our subjects throughout our teaching career. Too often teachers see themselves as having already mastered their subjects, or as knowing so much more about them than their students that further learning is unnecessary. However, there is no such thing as full mastery of a subject and the more we know about a subject the better our teaching will be. Further, as teachers we need to model for our students continued fascination with a subject and strategies for ongoing learning. Moreover, if we make continued learning a priority in our lives we will find teaching more fulfilling. Instead of dreading having to "teach that again" we will approach each class with the attitude: "What new things do I have to offer, and what new insights will I gain today?"

By their third year of teaching, many of the new teachers in our study saw the need for ongoing enhancement of their subject knowledge and appreciation. Anna spoke of the difficulty she had experienced teaching literacy because she "never loved literacy that much" (as distinct from science and math). Nina commented that in order to teach a subject well, "I have to make it interesting to me: if it's not interesting to me, I can't do it." Karen described how she constantly gathers knowledge for use with her students:

> Even when I'm not at school, when I'm watching TV, I'm thinking in the back of my mind, I can tell the kids about that . . . I try to look at the world through their eyes and think about making connections for them. So all the time I feel I'm learning how to be a better teacher. For example, I'm watching a show about how to renovate a house . . . and the only reason I'm watching it is because it tells me about how to build stable structures, how to put things together . . . And I never cared, but now I care because the kids want to know about it.

Marisa stated that teachers must acquire "a broader picture of what math can be" so they can give up the typical "rule-based, rote-based" approach to math and show students that math can be done "in a variety of ways." Similarly, Anita gave an example of how she can now teach math better because she understands it better.

> [Over the past three years], I've learned how to multiply. When I was a kid I learned how to multiply, but when I learned it again I learned it in terms of place value, and now I really understand what it is and can teach it to my students . . . . And every year I'm still learning, because I have to learn the content before I can learn or develop strategies for teaching it.

One thing we teachers need to learn increasingly about our subjects is how studying them can enrich *our* lives. If we cannot see this in our own case, how can we convince our students of the links to life, as discussed in Chapter 1? We should acknowledge – and even discuss with our students – how fortunate we are to be in a profession in which our daily work is potentially so rewarding at a personal level. Along these lines, Nina in year 3 observed that she has continued to develop as a teacher "because I'm a committed life-long learner myself . . . I want to know what's going on in the world." And Karen said:

I've always been a reader but I've never really been a writer, and I've only recently become aware that how you write has such a big impact on your reading . . . And now that I'm teaching writing, I'm becoming a more active reader and also a better writer than I was before, even though I've written a lot of papers. It's so stimulating. And sometimes when I'm reading to my daughter I'll say, "Oh my God, I've got to read this to the kids . . . Wow, look at the way the author put those words together. I can picture it perfectly in my mind." So yeah, I feel all the time that I'm developing as a teacher and as a person.

Pursue subject-specific pedagogical knowledge

Although subject content knowledge is clearly necessary for a teacher, subject specific *pedagogical* knowledge is also essential. Subject content and pedagogy are closely intertwined: we learn more about a subject as we learn how to teach it and vice versa. However, in theory the two are distinct, and frequently in the past the pedagogical aspect has been neglected. In addition to content knowledge, teachers need subject-specific knowledge about child development, student needs and interests, typical student difficulties and misunderstandings, effective teaching strategies and activities, and available pedagogical materials.

Taking knowledge of child development as an example, we should pursue it largely in relation to specific subjects. Too often in pre-service, child development is addressed in very general terms, the connection to pedagogy being assumed. For example, several new teachers in our study said they needed to know more about stages of reading development; notably, how we can interest grade 4–6 students in reading, now that they have acquired the basics of decoding. We also need to learn about exceptions to stage theories in relation to a particular subject: how children differ in their development in a subject and how we can accelerate knowledge of *that* subject in particular pupils.

We must also learn about textbooks, published learning materials, and school district programs in specific subject areas. Many of our graduates said they wished they knew more about their school district's programs when they began teaching. Vera commented: "There are so many programs and materials out there it's hard to sift through them all and know which ones will work in your classroom." Although there are challenges here, given that graduates go to different school districts, there are broad trends and similarities in the materials that student teachers can come to understand (as several of the study participants noted).

As well as trying to learn more about subject-specific pedagogy during pre-service, student teachers should develop plans for *ongoing* learning in this area. What is learned in initial training is just the tip of the iceberg. As Tanya said:

When I started, I didn't realize how little subject-specific knowledge I had . . . And the more I learn, the more I realize how much I need to learn . . . It takes a lot of dedication to get to the level you need, because you can certainly just come in and leave every day and get through just fine. But that's not the best way to do it.

We need the same attitude to subject pedagogy as to the subject itself: a passion to constantly learn more, both for our students' sake and our own. We should seek out workshops, courses, and professional literature, and join professional societies in our subject areas. Within our school, we need to get together with other teachers to discuss materials and pedagogy. Vera noted:

At my school we have an amazing in-service offering called the Curriculum Cafe, where we all get together for breakfast and people who have been at workshops present resources they have encountered and talk about them, telling us what is good, what is not, and how to use them. And I did this in my Reading Part 1 course as well: we all took a professional resource we had read and discussed what it stands for and how you can use it.

Implications for pre-service education

The above principles and strategies of subject teaching have significant implications for teacher education. We will discuss several of them in turn.

Use subject-specific knowledge as a basis for student admission and faculty hiring

Because subject content knowledge is so important, weight should be given to it when admitting teacher candidates. It should not be our only criterion, since other teacher qualities are also crucial; however, if other qualities are present, the more subject knowledge teachers have in relevant areas the richer their teaching will be. In hiring pre-service faculty, too, a major consideration should be knowledge of subject content and pedagogy, along with the ability to teach these at the pre-service level. We are dismayed when we see these qualifications almost entirely disregarded in hiring, especially when the new appointees are then immediately asked to do much of their instruction and supervision in subject-specific areas.

Emphasize subject content and pedagogy in the pre-service program

As noted earlier, pre-service programs in recent decades have tended to focus on broad issues and general pedagogy. Although general principles are obviously important, we believe that a more balanced position is required. General concepts and principles should be taught largely in the context of subject content and pedagogy, even in foundation courses. If we do not embed our general analyses and recommendations in subject material the danger is that new teachers will ignore them as they struggle to survive in the classroom and meet subject teaching expectations. An important move here is to organize much of our pre-service instruction in terms of a specific range of grade levels: for example, kindergarten through grade 6; grades 4 through 8; or the intermediate grades. Only in this way can we give adequate attention to subject-specific content, pedagogy, and child development.

Be selective in subject-specific instruction

Although we need to emphasize subject content in teacher education, not just any content will do. A weakness of traditional schooling has been excessive, superficial "coverage" of topics, and we must not replicate this in pre-service. We should explore key concepts, principles, skills, and method-ological approaches within a discipline, rather than just studying an array of isolated information. This in turn will help student teachers learn how to distinguish between more and less important subject matter. Another area in which prioritization and depth are essential is child development. This is a vast domain and attempting to deal with it in general courses leads to superficiality. Student teachers need specific information on developmental stages in the subject area(s) and at the age levels for which they are likely to be responsible. Insight into general principles of child development should largely emerge from such instruction.

Provide practicum experiences that foster subject-specific knowledge

Student teachers need to be in practicum placements where they see effective subject teaching in grades as close as possible to the level they are likely to teach at. Further, the approach to subject teaching must largely match what is being taught in the campus program. In order to maximize the value of the practicum, analysis of practicum experiences should take place back at the university campus, again with a strong subject emphasis. Videotaping can help here, not as in a "micro-teaching" approach – in which each step in the lesson is compared with a set procedure – but with open analysis and discussion of what was going on and why and how it might have been improved.

As far as possible, student teachers and cooperating teachers should be clustered together in a relatively small number of practicum schools. This facilitates visits by faculty and other supervisors, enables student teachers to support each other, and offers opportunities for the ongoing development of the cooperating teachers themselves. Clustering in a few schools means that we cannot always use the most effective individual teachers for practicum purposes, but we believe the advantages of this approach outweigh the disadvantages.

As faculty, continue to learn subject content and pedagogy

As pre-service faculty, we should work to increase our subject knowledge and interest, with the support of our program and the school of education. Forming subject groups among the faculty can greatly aid in this process. But we should also pursue professional development on our own, reading in our subject area(s) and attending subject-related courses, workshops, and conferences. As with school teachers, constant growth in subject matter knowledge among pre-service faculty not only improves instruction but makes our role more interesting and fulfilling. It also provides a model of teachers who are genuinely interested in their subject and keep on learning about it.

Initiate student teachers into ongoing growth in subject knowledge

Right from the beginning of the program, we should discuss with student teachers the importance of subject knowledge (both content and pedagogy) and how they will not have enough of it by the end of the program. Throughout the program student teachers should be introduced to ways of increasing their subject-specific knowledge – reading, courses, travel, movies, workshops, dialogue with pupils, and so on – and helped to develop concrete plans in this regard for the years ahead. We should note that enriching our lives in this way may appear self-indulgent but in fact has great pay-off for our pupils. Too often in teaching we give so much attention to lesson preparation that we do not have time to develop the knowledge and interests that ultimately make our teaching most effective.

Conclusion

Classroom teachers are required to spend most of their time teaching specific subjects such as literacy, math, science, and social studies. Other things being equal, the more they know about these subjects – and how to teach them – the more interesting and effective their teaching will be. As well as subject content knowledge, they need personal appreciation of subjects, the ability to select interesting and relevant topics within subjects, understanding of connections between subjects and to the "real world," knowledge of subject-specific child development and teaching methods and materials, and the attitudes and behaviors necessary for ongoing development of subject-specific knowledge and appreciation.

Subject-specific knowledge – both content and pedagogy – has tended to be neglected in teacher education in recent times. Although general theory and pedagogy are essential, a balance needs to be established between attention to general educational knowledge and subject-specific knowledge. Perhaps the most obvious way of doing this is to combine instruction in these two types of knowledge. Constructivism, inquiry, program planning, assessment, inclusion, collaboration, and other key educational topics should to a large extent be addressed in the context of subject-specific instruction.

Chapter 6

Professional identity

Over the three years of our study, a teacher's personal approach to the profession emerged as a high priority for teacher education. The 22 graduates we followed stressed such things as seeing the teacher's role broadly, taking a positive stance toward teaching, seeking help from – and collaborating with – other teachers, balancing work with personal life, and viewing themselves as continuing to grow professionally and personally. We were somewhat surprised at this emphasis on the total life and practice of the teacher (as distinct from instructional activities, narrowly conceived) but in fact it makes a great deal of sense. The teacher is not a mere "conduit" passing knowledge to the child (Connelly and Clandinin, 1999). As is often said, "we teach who we are": the whole person of the teacher is involved in the complex teaching–learning process. The teacher must personally embody the qualities of good teaching and learning if these are to become a reality in the classroom (Danielewicz, 2001).

In the long process of forging a professional identity, the first three years of teaching are an early stage. However, even at this point our study participants had much to say on the topic; and David, the teacher whose profile opens this chapter, exhibited an unusually strong sense of himself as a committed educator moving forward in the profession. This was partly the result of teaching experiences he had from his teenage years onward.

David

When I started teaching First Aid courses, I was 18 years old and the kids I was teaching were 14. Not a lot of age difference there. I came in and tried to be this authority figure. Well, I'm only four years older than these kids and I'm sure when I walked in the door, they spotted a phony and to be perfectly frank, they ate me alive. It was a very long, dragged-out course. We got through it but in that course I learned a lot.

Background

After completing his Bachelor of Arts degree, David immediately entered a two-year teacher credential program. In the three years that followed (the period of our study), he taught grade 7 in a middle- to upper-middle-class suburban school with a high percentage of ethnic minority students. The school district is very large and quite traditional, and tends to be prescriptive with respect to curriculum teaching materials.

David was fairly positive about his teacher education program, although he felt there were too many "busy work" assignments. He found the courses on legal issues and assessment particularly helpful.

> I felt well prepared to be in the profession. I think two years is a very good idea in terms of preparation. The practicums obviously – doing four – make you confident in your own developing style as a teacher and what you're going to do in the classroom.

He did three of his four practicums in the school that eventually hired him, including one semester in grade 7 when he and his mentor teacher held similar views on literacy instruction. In his first year of teaching he based his program on the one he had experienced during his practicum. "I started off with a long-range plan from the teacher who taught this grade last year and who I worked with as a student teacher." During his pre-service program David took a course on teaching English in middle school, but commented that it was not particularly helpful because the program advocated was not realistic for middle school students.

David's identity as a teacher

In our experience, it is rare to meet a beginning teacher as poised as David. He is self-assured, although recognizing he has much to learn. He cares about his students but has minimal classroom management issues. He focuses on pupil learning but also wants to foster a love of reading. His classroom is incredibly well organized but he aims to build a community. Many might be challenged by these tensions but David in his pragmatic approach reconciles them as just part of teaching.

David takes his work as a teacher seriously. As he commented at the end of his third year: "Teaching is not a 9 to 5 job, you are a teacher all the time. It is fundamentally your life – inside and outside the classroom." He feels that one of the essential qualities for being an effective teacher is "whole-hearted commitment." Nevertheless, he sees the need for teachers to look after themselves – indeed, enjoy themselves – if they are to survive:

There are times in this job when your principal is saying he needs such and such done; kids in the class are coming up and telling you they haven't done their homework; you've got a parent on the phone saying they don't understand the assignment and need more time; and you realize that it's May and in two weeks you have to start writing report cards. It's then that you need the ability to step back and just laugh . . . [And] these kids, if you let them, will make you laugh, they will entertain you . . . And you have to be able to enjoy yourself, otherwise you'll never get through it.

In defining himself as a teacher, David sees his job as ensuring success for all children: he strives to ensure that each student has a "personal best in grade 7." In all the interviews, he emphasized student learning, which he sees as his responsibility and as revolving around teaching the curriculum. Over time he feels less constrained by the formal curriculum expectations and the school district approved reading program, but he never strays far from a focus on teaching the curriculum.

Although aiming at success for all students, however, David is realistic about what he can do. In the pre-service program, "I had more of a global idealism that I could change the world." This has been tempered by recognizing that not all children will have the same achievements. "My goal now . . . is having every student . . . learn at their level." In general, David is now more aware of the constraints on academic teaching. At the end of year 3 he commented:

If there's one thing I would have liked to know about program planning it's that it doesn't come straight from the teacher's guide . . . You have to look at it and say okay, in reality, what can I do? Because, for example . . . my scheduled time for language arts is an hour, but by the time I start, it's quarter after, and then they have to do some seat work otherwise they're overloaded with homework. So you're talking about a 25- to 30-minute lesson. And one thing I've learned is that if I'm doing anything that's longer than 25–30 minutes, I should stop: for their sanity and mine. They're not going to absorb it, and I get panicked because I'm running out of time and start to speed up, and don't allow for questions.

David's identity as a teacher also includes being involved in all aspects of the school. He participates fully in the grade 7 and 8 divisional meetings, is on school-wide committees, is the union representative, and is very prominent in extra-curricular activities such as coaching. He believes that part of the reason parents respect him is his very visible presence coaching school teams.

Influences on David's professional identity

In studying David, we wanted to understand how a new teacher could have such a clear and strong sense of his professional identity. Over the three years, we noted three major influences.

Early teaching experiences

David is an extremely fit young man who has spent a lifetime involved in athletics. For over a decade he assumed different roles in aquatics programs in which, in his view, he acquired many skills for teaching. "The first thing I started doing was teaching little ones how to swim. You have a basic curriculum, front floats, back floats, etc." This evolved into his becoming "a First Aid and National Life Saving Society instructor where you teach people who are becoming life guards the skills they need." He now has 38 different certifications. David's long-term and continued involvement in aquatics influenced him as a teacher: maintaining the discipline of athletic training, aiming for personal bests, teaching skills, and focusing on safety. His success in aquatics gave him confidence that he could teach and, as the opening quote indicates, many opportunities to refine the craft of teaching and develop his self-image as a teacher.

Apprenticeship in the school

David's three practicums as a student teacher in the school in which he was ultimately hired eased his transition into teaching. During practice teaching he established relationships with the teachers, in particular those teaching grades 7 and 8; they work as a team (e.g., developing a behavior code for all students) and they welcomed him onto the team even as a student teacher. "The support from the teachers is there. If I ask them a question I'll find an answer. But they don't say this is what you should do in terms of your literacy program, they don't micromanage in that way." In turn he feels he has influenced them by providing in-services on new curriculum documents, as we describe later.

David works closely with another new teacher who also teaches grade 7, splitting some teaching responsibilities; this eases the demands of program planning. When observing his class, we noted that this colleague wanders into the classroom and asks a question or figures out scheduling details (e.g., the time for an assembly). They have a very easy and collegial relationship. The Junior Literacy Coordinator helped David set up his program and hired him to be an instructor in the Summer Literacy Camp. He describes her as "a walking encyclopedia of literacy." In his first year he said: "I'll tell her how I want to approach a unit and she'll fine-tune it, or give me some things to think about, or come back and say: That's good; can you take it to this level?" By the second year he was "more likely to try it on my own. If it didn't work, I would go back and say, okay, this is what I did, this is what happened; and then see what feedback she had for me." The various forms of mentorship improved his teaching, especially reducing the problems of classroom management that can undermine a beginning teacher's confidence.

Early leadership opportunities

Interestingly, David became involved in two major district-wide committees in his second year of teaching. This happened partly by chance: while attending a district-sponsored workshop he was invited by one of the facilitators to join the committees. For one committee, he had to develop a working knowledge of the document *Think Literacy*, which focuses on comprehension strategies; he had to teach particular strategies to his class, collect samples of student work, and then lead in-services for teachers. On the second committee – the diversity writing team – he was required to develop curriculum for teaching a particular novel. (In addition, David was approached by a publisher to be a demonstration teacher for a video they were making of their new literacy program, and he was videotaped teaching literacy strategies to his class.) Doing professional development sessions for experienced teachers could have been daunting for a new teacher, but David was in a very supportive team environment. As the committees worked together conducting many in-service sessions, he began to see himself as a leader and teachers in turn saw him as leader. David knew early in his career that he wanted to be in educational leadership (he would like one day to become a principal); having a sense of his career trajectory, then, he welcomes these leadership opportunities because they match the vision he has for himself. He intends to complete his principal certification courses as soon as possible.

Beyond deepening his knowledge of curriculum, the committee work has introduced him to many outstanding teachers and consultants. He commented at the end of his third year that "disillusionment is a collective state of being for teachers." After 10 years of school funding reductions and brutal attacks on teachers by the government in the media, there is a "collective pessimism." Through his leadership work, he has connected with many who have a brighter outlook towards teaching and higher morale. He thoughtfully commented: "If you are surrounded by negativity it is hard not to get snowballed into it." The networking let him "hear other voices and be introduced to educators doing other things," which has helped him retain his optimistic view of teaching.

David's class in action

David's grade 7 classroom is extremely well ordered and tidy. There is student work on display; a chart with the code of behavior is prominently placed at the front of the room; homework notices are posted; and the furniture is arranged in a U shape so everyone focuses on the front of the room. When the bell rings, the students enter the class and immediately turn their attention to getting organized for work. There is quiet chatting as they sort through their materials. In the first period, the language arts lesson involves reading a story about the adventurer John Goddard from the textbook *Sightlines*. Students take turns reading aloud, all are engaged, and many respond to questions posed by David. There is a quick review of strategies that can be used for synthesizing information and drawing inferences from text. Students then answer a question from the textbook, which requires them to identify three pieces of advice implied in the story of John Goddard and organize them in a paragraph. All students are on task and work quietly for almost 30 minutes. The next period is history, and the class is studying a crucial era in early Canadian history. Again, the students use the textbook, with David reading the text and adding many fascinating details that help "history come alive." All the students are attentive and on task. The history lesson is repeated after recess with the other grade 7 class.

Next steps

David's experiences in teaching to date have been very positive, with a close match between his ideal and the reality, a sense that his pupils are learning, a feeling that he is respected by his colleagues, and many opportunities to exercise leadership. His view of the role of the teacher is in line with his pedagogy, classroom organization, and extra-curricular activities, thus creating a seamless practice.

David had planned to switch grades in his fourth year and teach a combined grade 5/6 class in the same school; however, while we were on site during one of our year 3 visits he was offered a position in a local high school as a Career Path teacher, working with at-risk youth. He was extremely excited about this new challenge, recognizing that he would have much to learn. He was recently granted admission to a doctoral program on educational leadership but had to decline because of the high tuition cost. He intends to re-apply once he is in a better financial situation. It will be interesting to continue following David, a young man with great potential, a commitment to education, an optimistic yet realistic outlook, and a strong sense of direction in his career.

What and why of professional identity

By professional identity we mean how teachers perceive themselves professionally. It includes their sense of their goals, responsibilities, style, effectiveness, level of satisfaction, and career trajectory. New teachers' initial identity comes from a variety of sources: for example, internalization of societal views of the profession (Kennedy, 2005); memories of their own teachers' practices when they were in school (Lortie, 1975); and prior notions about what they will be able to achieve, often based more on youthful optimism than experience and research. As they engage in pre-service preparation and begin full-time teaching, they have an opportunity to refine their identity considerably. They do this largely by learning more about the possibilities and realities of teaching, but also by making individual decisions about the kind of teacher they wish to be. Teachers in similar school and classroom settings often adopt rather different approaches to their role, depending on their distinctive personality, interests, abilities, and life circumstances.

Why is it important for teachers to explore and develop their professional identity? A key reason is to hone a professional self-image that supports effective teaching and gives them a positive view of their contribution. For example, teachers sometimes have too narrow a view of their role. They need to become aware of the complexity of their work, including such elements as getting to know their students, tailoring instruction to the diverse needs of students, fostering understanding of complex and changing concepts, teaching attitudes toward life and learning, and building a class culture that facilitates students' academic learning and personal and social growth. Developing such a view not only enables teachers to be more effective but also gives them greater pride and motivation in the profession.

Another reason for teachers to work on their identity is to optimize the relationship between their professional and personal lives. Although it is legitimate to speak – as we do – of "professional identity," we should be aware that no sharp separation exists between the professional and the personal. As Hagger and McIntyre (2006) say:

> Thoughtful commentators on the teaching profession . . . have noted how closely teachers' personal and professional identities tend to be intertwined . . . Most teachers find that their individual humanity and the totality of their human experience are essential resources on which they draw as classroom teachers.
>
> (p. 55)

Teachers must decide how much of themselves to bring to the profession and in what ways. "Being professional" often has connotations of *separating* professional action from personal motivation; but in fact bringing the two together in certain (though not all) respects can have advantages both for teachers and their students. Professionally, it can enable teachers to harness their personal interests and talents, thus increasing their energy and effectiveness and making them role models of people who are passionate about learning and life generally. At a personal level, such convergence can mean that teachers experience greater well-being as they attain key life goals *in the context of* their work. As Karen said in her third year of teaching: "Now that I'm teaching writing, I'm becoming a more active reader and also a better writer . . . So yeah, I feel all the time that I'm developing as a teacher and as a person."

A further reason for teachers to attend to their professional identity is to add an explicit directional aspect to their career. Teachers should not just see themselves in the present but as moving forward in the profession (as we noted in David's profile). They need to be conscious of the limitations of their pre-service preparation, no matter how well conducted, and view themselves as embarking on a career-long program of professional learning, one that will increase their effectiveness and deepen the satisfaction they gain from teaching. Also, if they wish, they should develop plans for taking on new leadership roles within the school and beyond. Teachers vary in how long they can continue to sustain the heavy psychological and even physical demands of everyday teaching. Building on their rich classroom experience, they may go on to other positions in education such as school administration, school district resource work, and pre-service and in-service teacher education.

Problems of professional identity

A major problem in the area of teacher identity is the tendency, already mentioned, to define teaching too narrowly. "Your job is to teach," teachers are often told, that is, to foster *academic* learning; other roles, if noted at all, are not emphasized. Even some teachers have difficulty accepting a broader view of the profession: "I trained to be a teacher," some say; "why should I have to listen to them talk about their life outside the school?" But most teachers soon see (in varying degrees) the necessity of other roles, such as relating to individual students, building class community, and fostering life skills. Student teachers need more guidance and support than they currently receive in incorporating these roles into their professional practice and identity.

A second difficulty is that the intellectual depth and knowledge of teachers is often underestimated, despite the fact that they have at least one university degree – often two or three – have read widely, and are intelligent, talented people. University researchers tend to talk down to teachers, "inservicing them" with little acknowledgement of their insights and experience (Cochran-Smith and Lytle, 1993; Zeichner, 1995; Zeichner and Noffke, 2001). Parents and other members of the public frequently accuse them of making very obvious mistakes in carrying out their job. Finally, for reasons difficult to comprehend, the fact that teachers work with children frequently leads to their being seen as having a low level of intellectual sophistication. In an important sense teachers are "infantilized" by the system and society (Barth, 1990, p. 36), and they can easily buy into this identity themselves.

In contrast to the discounting of teachers' abilities, there is the further problem of teachers being viewed (and viewing themselves) as authority figures, distanced from their pupils: "the sage on the stage." This image is often supported by parents, colleagues, and even pupils themselves. Teachers who acknowledge that they need to learn more, and in particular that they sometimes learn with and from their students, are in danger of losing respect. The status of being primarily a knowledgeable expert is gratifying and may be difficult to give up. Teachers must be helped to see that combining being an expert with a relational, interactive role can have even greater rewards, including a satisfying rapport with students, more effective and enjoyable teaching, and their own continued intellectual and professional growth.

Yet another problem (found in other "helping professions" as well) is that teachers frequently see themselves as a kind of servant, helping others without necessarily receiving much in return: self-sacrifice is a given. When teachers try to resist this outlook they often feel guilty. Of course, the other-oriented, caring nature typical of those who enter teaching is admirable, and is essential to the rapport they establish with their students and their capacity to survive and thrive in a profession with such heavy interpersonal demands. But a balance is needed in which responsibility for caring for students is shared with the class community, parents, the local community, and others. Teachers need to look after themselves to a significant extent if they are to survive, remain strong, grow personally, and continue to be there for their students.

Finally, there is the problem of the "super-teacher" syndrome: seeing oneself as able to "work wonders" in children's lives (Kosnik, 1999). Teachers need to be realistic about the challenges they face, especially given the inequality of life circumstances in society, the widespread inadequacy of funding for schooling, and the constraints inherent in the classroom situation (Kennedy, 2005). A paradox of teaching is that we have enormous impact on students and yet there is always room for increased effectiveness; we can improve substantially every year for 30 years but still have far to go. Teachers' impact should be documented and celebrated, but the limits to what can be achieved at a given stage must also be acknowledged (Kennedy, 2006).

Principles and strategies of professional identity

We argued earlier that it is important for teachers to have a sense of identity. However, some self-perceptions are better than others: we need to explore which elements are more appropriate and helpful for a teacher. Further, we must consider ways in which these elements may be developed and enhanced. The following are principles and strategies of identity formation that we think are especially relevant at this time.

See teaching in broad terms

As noted before, effective teaching requires working on many fronts at once; famously, a teacher has to be good at multi-tasking. Kennedy (2006) states:

> [T]eaching is a multifaceted activity. By that I mean that teachers routinely do more than one thing at a time . . . I recently interrogated teachers about their practices and found that their practices reflect their concerns about six different things: (a) covering desirable content, (b) fostering student learning, (c) increasing student willingness to participate, (d) maintaining lesson momentum, (e) creating a civil classroom community, and (f) attending to their own cognitive and emotional needs.
>
> (p. 205)

To these six might be added other key components, such as listening carefully to students' views and developing a good teacher–student relationship. Obviously, then, if teachers are to be optimally effective in their work, they must include all these tasks (and more besides) as part of their self-perception.

Having a broad approach to teaching may appear to be a burden; but in fact, as discussed before, it makes our work more manageable and fulfilling. For example, getting to know our students well helps us when planning learning activities. Building class community facilitates group work and classroom management, and makes classroom interaction more enjoyable for students and teachers alike. Frequent pupil assessment, if done in a feasible way, helps both with report writing and program planning. Discussing life issues increases motivation and improves our rapport with students. Addressing the "multiliteracies" of home and community supports our interaction both with students and their parents.

The new teachers in our study increasingly saw the need for a broad teaching role and seemed willing to accept it as part of their professional identity. For example, Wanda commented that "teaching is no longer just knowing subject matter; it's also knowing psychology, and social work, and classroom management, and peer management techniques: how to work with colleagues." According to Sophia, although in a sense she prepares students for standardized tests, her main concern is to give them "strategies for life . . . strategies they will not only be using for test writing but also in life, to figure out solutions to problems." Marisa said:

> What I want [my students] to remember from their experience is that they were welcomed, they felt safe, and they had fun; I want them to

learn a lot, but I tell them all the time that I first of all want them to become cooperative, helpful human beings who get along with other people, know how to make friends and be a friend, and so on.

Be realistic about the challenges of teaching

According to Labaree (2004), "teaching is an extraordinarily difficult form of professional practice. It is grounded in the necessity of motivating cognitive, moral, and behavioral change in a group of involuntary and frequently resistant clients" (pp. 55–56). Those who suggest that teachers have an easy time of it because of their "short work day" and summer break have no understanding of the reality. Apart from the fact that the actual work day is long, the great majority of teachers feel drained at the end of the day and week, and could not possibly get through the year without the prospect of an annual time to regroup and refresh themselves. Many parents heave a sigh of relief when they send their two or three children off to school at the end of the summer, whereas teachers have to manage 25 or 30 often very challenging students all day for 10 months. And apart from these demands, they face the added stresses of inadequate facilities and resources, external control measures that run counter to sound teaching, and constant uninformed criticism from many quarters. Teachers need to acknowledge and come to terms with all this as they develop their professional identity.

Among our study participants, John reported having to "adjust to the workload" in his first year. "I've always been a worker . . . but . . . I was overtaken by the actual workload . . . it seems like I breathe, live, and eat school, and sometimes it's overwhelming." At the end of her second year, Felicity said she continued to find teaching very demanding.

> Teaching is a lot harder than I thought it would be . . . it takes a lot more stamina and patience than I thought possible . . . [T]he cold, hard reality is that in your first years of teaching, and maybe even after that, it's almost like you're slinging in the mud pits. Honestly, you get thrown to the wolves . . . I know I'm going to stay in it because that's what I want to do, it's my resolve. But I can see why some people might be unsure.

Nina spoke eloquently about how demanding teaching is, while also (like Felicity) expressing her commitment to it.

> Basically, you need to go into teaching knowing that you're going to work your rear end off, you're not going to earn a lot of money, and often you're not going to get a lot of support. But you do it because you love it.

In their third year, many of the participants still found teaching very challenging in a number of ways. A few even mentioned facing criticism from their colleagues for "showing them up" by working too hard. Several talked of getting tired, of needing to ease up, and of having to revise their ideas about how much one can achieve as a teacher. Jody spoke of inadequate salaries, increased paper work, and governments "downloading everything onto teachers [so that] the fun stuff is falling away." Felicity said: "I'm a little more conservative now. If I have one or two students I've seen incredible growth in . . . then I'm satisfied with that; and I think that's realistic." Paul, who taught special needs students in a very low socioeconomic area, observed:

> It's hard when you're trying to help so much but everyone is treating you so badly: parents are not being respectful and students are treating you horribly. You think, How dare they? . . . But then you realize that some of them don't want your help. They need it badly, but they're going to react as if they don't want it. So I've learned that you can't just come in with idealism and good ideas . . . You need to be realistic, knowing that certain communities have big challenges. You have to accept them and . . . figure out what's going to work with this group.

And Maria commented: "I'm sometimes frustrated, but at the end of the day I go home and still have a smile on my face. So I know this is for me . . . It's killing me, but it's a great job!"

Take a strong, positive stance toward teaching

According to Connelly and Clandinin (1999), teachers' identities are composed by the "narratives" that shape their working lives. Such identities are often "held with conviction and tenacity": teachers may even "resign and search for different employment" if they cannot express their life narrative in their work (p. 94). Teachers take such a strong stance because they have a positive view of teaching. They believe that with the right pedagogy and classroom atmosphere, their students can find the school experience satisfying, learn a great deal, and grow as human beings. At a personal level, too, they believe that, despite the challenges of teaching, they can forge a viable, fulfilling profession for themselves.

In line with this perspective, all our study participants reported success and fulfillment in their first three years of teaching. Although realistic about the difficulties, they spoke of considerable achievement and satisfaction. Some may not stay in the profession in the longer term, in part because of the frustrations; the capacity to deal with the challenges of teaching varies with individual personality and circumstances. But all showed awareness of how much their students learned and of their own professional status and worth, even where this was not acknowledged by outsiders.

For example, Paul in his second year spoke of his refusal to approach teaching in the manner so often proposed by governments and school districts.

> The focus [in literacy] is now very much on accountability: they want to make sure you're assessing and collecting data and then showing an improvement the next time. And there's nothing wrong with assessing and keeping track of things, but the *way* it's being done is bureaucratic – a "bean counter" approach – as opposed to seeing whether these kids are actually getting something out of their schooling, or whether I'm now spending all my time assessing and collecting data instead of planning a writing assignment for struggling students, or whatever.

David, also in his second year, described how he is taking a stronger stand on how he goes about teaching. "[I'm now] more confident to try new things, a lot more experimental with my teaching and willing to bring in my own concepts. I've got a better idea of what's important and what's not . . . I focus more on those important things that help the students, filtering out the excess."

On this foundation of a positive and confident approach to their work, teachers can see the talents they have developed and how much they are accomplishing. Liane in her second year said:

> [R]ight now I think I'm doing the best English teaching I've done so far in my career . . . I'm able to combine teaching literary elements with the major social issues that the [novel we're studying] deals with; and the kids are very much into it.

Maria also spoke of how she was more on top of things by the end of her second year. "I feel there's been an improvement in every area." Tanya in her third year reported: "I have a lot more confidence in what I can do in grade 4 . . . As April and May come, I see how much they've improved over the school year." Jeannie, also in her third year, commented:

> I think I make a big difference, especially in a school like ours where a lot of the parents are on shift work and not necessarily spending a ton of time with their children . . . This year in grade 3 it's been neat because six of my students I taught in grade 1, so I see how they've grown and changed.

Seek help and collaborate

In a large research study across many schools, Lortie (1975) found that teachers "turn to one another for assistance and consider such peer help their most important source of assistance" (p. 76). Edwards and Collison (1996) see teaching as "a community of practice in which all participants are learning and at the same time shaping the understandings that operate within the community" (p. 30). Similarly, Hammerness, Darling-Hammond, and Bransford (2005) state that "the knowledge teachers need to teach well . . . is constructed collectively within local and broader communities" (p. 383). Connelly and Clandinin (1999) maintain that teachers' identities are "communally sustained as people support one another through confirmation of their beliefs, values, and actions and as they share stories and recollections" (p. 101).

In their first year, a large proportion of our study participants stressed the importance of going to other teachers for help. Anita said she would advise a beginning teacher to "try to gather as many resources as possible and maybe sit in on a few different teachers' classrooms to see how they are run, to get some ideas." Heather proposed saying to new teachers:

> Talk to as many experienced teachers as possible, because the teachers in the school have so many resources . . . If you're teaching primary, try to talk to the primary teachers . . . nobody has everything but you can get a bit from here and there . . . And those things are all tested, that's the good thing . . . they have already used them in their own classroom.

Paul felt that looking to other teachers for help was important not just for beginners but for all teachers:

> A key thing for a new teacher – well, any teacher – is to get out there and talk to other teachers. You get tired and stressed and just feel like holing up in your room . . . but that's the worst thing you can do.

Similarly, Tanya suggested that teachers will always need to be asking questions of their colleagues:

> [Y]ou're going to continue to have questions for many, many years and you [must] keep asking. I talked to one teacher around the corner who is retiring, and I asked her "How do you do that?" and she said "Oh, it's hard. It's just hard." And it's interesting to talk to someone who's been in the profession for 30 years and who's saying, "Yes, it's a challenge, and yes, I still ask that question too, and we're doing the best we can, and this is the way I do it."

Apart from simply seeking help, many of the interviewees saw the need for regular collaboration with other teachers, whether in pairs, in teams, or at a whole-school level. Among other things, they thought this was important to ensure a common approach in a particular grade or set of grades or across the school. Paul strongly emphasized "sharing" in schools, noting that

> in one of our division meetings, we went around and did a survey of what different teachers have in their rooms, and other school resources . . . And I know it's hard for groups of people to get along and work together . . . but I think that should be our goal.

Wanda talked of having a common "vision" in a school, rather than "everybody coming at it from different angles." She said that if you have "a cohesive team and a team approach, then it makes it a lot easier for the students. They know what to expect going forward [to later grades]." In March of her second year, Vera commented on how much she had appreciated working in a team, by contrast with her first year when at times it was "pretty rocky" and "really lonely."

Look after yourself

Teachers need to pay attention to their own well-being if they are to survive and have the energy to help their students in the long term. They also have to live a balanced life – to the extent possible – if they are to model a sound way of life for their students and give helpful input in classroom discussion of life issues. According to Connelly and Clandinin (1999), teachers' satisfaction with their work is closely related to maintenance of their identity, and they believe it is possible – and legitimate – for teachers to adapt their teaching "in a way that is sensitive to the question of who [they] are" (p. 102). Once again, the personal and professional are connected.

Many of the new teachers we studied thought it essential to attend to their own well-being, despite their hectic work schedule. John said he would advise new teachers to take time for themselves, find people who can support them, and "practice what they preach" about balanced living. Paul in his first year noted that "teaching is like any profession where you're giving yourself, so to speak, and have to make sure you're not giving yourself away too quickly. It has to be sustainable." At the end of his third year, he reported:

> Because my class was especially hard [this year], I learned by February not to think about it when I left the building . . . I knew the only way I was going to get through the year was to go home and totally forget

about it . . . [C]ompared with previous years, I really had a weekend, I really had an evening, I went home and didn't think about stuff.

Marisa, also at the end of her third year, talked about how she is achieving a better "home–work balance":

> I'm getting better at it. I've given myself more permission, especially in the last couple of months, to watch TV at 9:00 at night if I want to, rather than planning until 10:30 as I did in the first couple of years. And I'm realizing that things will be okay tomorrow if I don't spend that extra half hour planning. That comes partly from experience: getting better at seeing what needs to be done and how long it will take.

A common theme in the interviews was that teachers should not "beat up on themselves" or expect too much of themselves. Karen observed that mistakes are a natural part of the learning process:

> Second-year teaching is still hard, but I'm trying to think of myself as a work in progress. I'm learning new things every day, and not expecting to do things perfectly . . . And I think it's a positive attitude because the kids are also learning new things every day. And if they make comments about my not doing something perfectly, or making a mistake, I bring it back to that's how learning is, we all make mistakes and still have things to learn.

Many advocated making things manageable by implementing just one or two innovations at a time. Candice reported:

> In my first year I said to myself, I'm going to make the language program my major focus and everything else will be icing on the cake . . . And then this year I've largely kept my math and language programs from last year and focused on science and social studies.

Sophia in her third year said:

> I came out of teachers college . . . wanting to do it all. But I now realize that I'm building my program a bit at a time: I can't do it all in one year . . . I have these visions, but each year I play with it and mix it up a bit . . . I do the best I can.

Grow professionally

Continued professional growth is important both to increase our effectiveness and to make teaching more fulfilling. Snow, Griffin, and Burns (2006) say that ongoing development is necessary because "teacher knowledge is incomplete at the end of the pre-service preparation" (p. x). They argue for rejecting the "status-shift" view of teacher development, according to which pre-service teacher education leads to "sharp shifts in status and hypothesized accompanying shifts in capacity" (p. 5). As Jody, one of our new teachers, observed in her third year: "You always have to learn. My education is not finished, it's ongoing. Even if I was teaching grade 1 every year, it's an ongoing thing. Professional development is so important."

All the new teachers in our study spoke in varying degrees about their experiences of professional development. This often involved professional reading and taking workshops and courses, but many also found significant opportunities for growth in their own classroom and school. Karen commented:

> I just want to keep learning . . . to learn more and more, so that next year it becomes easier and I have more strategies. I want to keep challenging myself and talking to my colleagues and learning from their experience.

Liane said:

> Every day I notice things that, if I was to do them again, I would do differently; and I take note of those things all of the time. And the way things are happening in my class this year is very different from last year.

Paul observed:

> I'm constantly learning about things I need to know. I'm reading, going to workshops . . . But even just talking to people, and just thinking, having time to go, "Oh, this is a direction I need to go in." . . . There are definitely useful things I pick up [from professional reading]. But really it's more looking at the students and thinking, "Okay, what do they need right now? And can I provide it? And how can I provide it?"

Develop a sense of career trajectory

Lortie (1975) points out that, "[c]ompared with most other kinds of middle-class work, teaching is relatively 'career-less.' There is less opportunity for the movement upward which is the essence of career" (p. 84). The status of a new, young teacher "is not appreciably different from that of the highly experienced old-timer" (p. 85). To the extent that movement is possible (e.g., by becoming a principal or guidance counselor), it can often result in the virtual loss of one's identity as a teacher: the mobility may be scarcely *within* teaching at all. It is to be hoped that solutions to this problem will be found in the future. In the meantime, much depends on individual teachers fashioning a career path for themselves. For example:

- becoming an increasingly strong and well-informed teacher, a "master" teacher
- becoming a "lead teacher" or "resource teacher" in one's school
- becoming an educational writer while still teaching (like Vivian Paley or Nancie Atwell)
- doing part-time pre-service or in-service teaching (which may later become full-time)
- becoming a principal who to a significant degree is a curriculum leader in the school
- starting an alternative school of some sort, whether public or private.

Many of the new teachers in our study already had ideas about potential career trajectories for themselves. For example, John in his second year commented:

> [In the future, I will] largely continue what I'm doing, enjoying that I'm a teacher, teaching grade 3 . . . and also get different experiences under my belt. Progressively, however, I would like to . . . go back and get my master's . . . and maybe start moving around a bit, teaching grade 1 and eventually grade 6 . . . And I would be interested in moving towards teaching at a school of education one day.

Nina, though a highly energetic and committed teacher, remarked in her second year: "I don't want to be a classroom teacher all my life . . . [I]n the long term . . . my sights are on doing other things with my degree and my experience."

Marisa in her second year spoke mainly about filling immediate gaps in her knowledge, for example in math teaching and long-range planning. However, by her third year she was looking further ahead:

> The more I teach, the more I realize that I love teaching language – reading, writing, and so on. And I enjoy working with my ESL students as well. So I'm thinking about maybe in the future teaching ESL or even perhaps working as a teacher librarian. But I'd have to do my qualifications, so those are more long-term goals.

Felicity at the end of her third year had rather firm ideas about her future, especially about what would *not* be appropriate for her:

I went back to school as a mature student [and] I don't think I could actually survive 20 years in a classroom. I don't mean that in a negative way, but it really is so tiring . . . and I don't want to be in the classroom if I'm exhausted and crabby . . . I thought a bit about administration, but if you think teaching is hard, you really have to be a special person to go into administration. So I'm thinking rather of curriculum development or teacher education, down the road.

Implications for pre-service education

We now explore some of the implications of the foregoing sections for pre-service education. In doing so, our focus shifts from the role of the classroom teacher to that of the teacher educator attempting to foster professional identity.

Help student teachers develop and personalize a conception of teaching

Central to preparing teachers is helping them develop a sound overall conception of teaching. For professional identity formation, a further step is required: student teachers need an image of themselves as implementing that conception of teaching. They must commit both to a mode of teaching and a mode of being (Danielewicz, 2001; Hammerness et al., 2005). In our opinion, we must help them see themselves in a broad role that includes, for example, curriculum decision making, classroom organization, community building, and developing a good teacher–student relationship. We can explore with them the conceptions of teaching they bring from their own experience of schooling. We can read press clippings together and watch movies (e.g., *Mr. Holland's Opus*, *Dead Poets Society*), discussing and critiquing popular images of teachers such as the super-teacher, the bleeding heart teacher, and the sage on the stage.

In these discussions, teacher educators should not just be neutral facilitators. We should encourage student teachers to adopt a broadly constructivist or progressivist pedagogy and a corresponding self-identity. We should recommend that they pursue balance in their life, to the extent feasible, developing *a good way of life* in which their teaching role is an integral component. We should emphasize that health and family matters have high priority, and show that we mean this in the way we interact with them and run the program. Socializing within the cohort should be encouraged and constantly working until the small hours of the morning should be discouraged. In the practicum schools, we must make clear to both cooperating teachers and student teachers that we do not favor "throwing student teachers in the deep end."

Embody a sound professional identity in the pre-service program

It is not enough to discuss and advocate a teacher identity; we must ensure that it is embodied in the pre-service program. We should create a program climate in which identities flourish (Danielewicz 2001), a climate characterized by openness, dialogue, collaboration, and agency. We need to set a respectful tone, so student teachers come to see themselves as worthy of respect and agency. We must have genuine discussions with our student teachers, in which we are clearly open to learning from them. When possible, we should negotiate the curriculum with them (e.g., the nature and timing of assignments). We should provide them with opportunities to do research, both in our large-scale projects and in their own self-studies of practice.

Not only should we foster this way of being a teacher, we should also explicitly share with our student teachers our own vision and identity as teacher educators, outlining the choices we have made and continue to make on a daily basis. "Sharing the secrets" in this way will be instructive in itself and in addition enable them to get more out of the program. In this regard, Labaree (2004) observes:

> Most professionals rent their expertise without disclosing its mysteries, so they can reserve its power to themselves. But teachers are different . . . The aim is to enable students to get on with life under their own steam . . . In the same manner, teacher educators are in the business of demystifying teaching, giving away their own expertise in order to empower the prospective teacher to carry on the practice of teaching without need for continuous consultation and chronic professional dependency.
>
> (pp. 60–61)

We teacher educators must also model being professionals who work together. We should engage in collaborative practice, discuss the value of working as team, have assignments that cross course boundaries, have a schedule for assignments so they don't bunch up too much, and develop a largely common vision that pervades the program. As Lortie (1975) says: "Unless students in training can experience at least some sense of collegiality – some sharing of technical problems and alternative solutions – they will be ill-prepared for such efforts when they work alongside one another" (p. 66).

Explore the realities of teaching

Student teachers have to understand the realities of teaching and come to terms with them at a personal level. They must see themselves not as conquering heroes but as grappling with the challenges of teaching (nevertheless finding it satisfying, all things considered). According to Lortie (1975): "Utopian statements of intent probably press teachers back to conservative, relatively concrete outcomes; they discourage the risk-taking required for creativity" (p. 233). Far from giving a sense of the realities of teaching, teacher education programs often feed into student teachers' excessive idealism (Kennedy, 2006), and when faced with the realities teachers often respond "by going into reverse" (Hagger and McIntyre, 2006, p. 56). By contrast, student teachers need to be helped to "come to terms rationally with the complex problems of relating their roles as teachers to themselves as persons" (Hagger and McIntyre, 2006, p. 56).

Of course, student teachers can only fully understand the realities of teaching and how to deal with them when they become regular teachers. However, more could be done during the pre-service program, both by providing information on campus and through well-designed practicum experiences. As mentioned earlier, student teachers need opportunities to go beyond the "visiting performer" role and see teaching from their cooperating teacher's point of view. Also, practicums should be spread throughout the year so they have a chance to discuss their experiences with each other and with the faculty. As Hammerness et al. (2005) say:

> [T]eacher educators need to make sure that candidates have opportunities to practice and reflect on teaching *while enrolled in their preparation programs*. During both the pre-service period and initial years in the field, new teachers need support in interpreting their experiences and expanding their repertoire, so they can continue to learn how to become effective rather than infer the wrong lessons from their early attempts at teaching.
>
> (p. 375)

Lay the groundwork for ongoing teacher development

One of the main tasks of initial teacher education is to prepare student teachers "for a situation in which they will need to go on learning" (Hagger and McIntyre, 2006, p. 6). According to Bransford, Darling-Hammond, and LePage (2005), teacher preparation is far from complete at the end of the pre-service program, and teacher educators must focus on providing new teachers with "the core ideas and broad understandings of teaching and learning that give them traction on their later development" (p. 3).

Part of what is involved here is helping student teachers see that "a high level of . . . expertise cannot be attained quickly" (Hagger and McIntyre, 2006, p. 6). However, Hagger and McIntyre, along with Hammerness et al. (2005), are critical of stage theories that suggest that the developmental path teachers follow is relatively uniform. The starting points and growth patterns vary greatly, and much can be done to speed up development.

It is important, however, not to focus too much on *formal* methods of professional development: courses, workshops, formal mentoring programs. Hagger and McIntyre (2006) say that teachers learn "primarily on their own initiative and on the basis of their own classroom experience" (p. 6). New teachers are extremely busy, and formal in-service programs, although they can be very helpful, are sometimes disappointing (as several of our study participants reported). Moreover, emphasizing them too much can exaggerate the role of the external "expert" in teacher development (Zeichner, 1995). As well as giving substantial weight to outside activities, we must help student teachers acquire the concepts, attitudes, and methods they need to achieve significant professional learning in their own school and classroom and through their own professional reading and inquiry.

Conclusion

By professional identity we mean teachers' overall perception of themselves as professionals. This self-perception should be quite broad. Teachers need to understand that a wide array of tasks are involved in helping students succeed in school and in life, and they must willingly embrace this broad role. This does not mean they have to sacrifice themselves. On the contrary, adopting a broad approach to teaching leads to greater professional success and satisfaction. Moreover, it is legitimate for teachers to approach their profession in a way that is personally feasible and helps them flourish as human beings. Only in this way will they be able to survive as teachers, continue to be there for their students, and model a way of life that is instructive and inspiring to their students.

In pre-service education, we should aim to help student teachers understand and accept their broad role and achieve a sound integration of the personal and professional. We should inform them about the challenges of teaching, but enable them to see how they can be effective and fulfilled despite these challenges. We need to set them on a path of continued professional growth, taking advantage of formal in-service programs but also opportunities to learn in their own classroom and school. In the pre-service program itself, we should model and embody a sound work–life balance, giving student teachers the respect and support they need to develop a strong and optimistic approach to the profession.

Chapter 7

A vision for teaching

Finally, the new teachers in our study gave high priority to having a general teaching approach or philosophy, what we here call a "vision" for teaching. Being helped to develop such a vision was one of the things they appreciated most in their pre-service program. Sophia reported that "what my teacher education program did for me was help foster my philosophy, and my philosophy is what makes me the teacher I am: it is more important than any learning activity they taught me. Their philosophy was very collaborative and nurturing, and revolved around multiple intelligences." Wanda said that her pre-service instructors exposed her to "a very good general approach in terms of how to work language and literature into your teaching." And Tanya commented:

> There is no way [the pre-service faculty] could have taught everything we needed from September to June for every grade level and every situation. But I think they gave us the philosophy we needed to make our way through our first year.

When they were critical of this aspect of the pre-service program, it was not because they thought it was unimportant but because it was sometimes not well handled. As we saw in the Introduction, some felt the approach or philosophy advocated was not explained clearly enough or with sufficient indication of its practical implications.

To give an initial sense of what we mean by a vision for teaching we present the case of Marisa, a study participant who seemed to us to have an especially clear, sound, and integrated understanding of what she was striving for as a teacher. Her profile illustrates how a vision embraces both general goals and specific ideas about program planning and classroom culture and organization.

Marisa

> You must have clear goals, you must know where you're going, and you build your lessons on that. I think that's what adds to my stress because

> I spend so much time planning my lessons, and planning where I'm going to go. It's not just the day before, with me thinking, "Okay, what am I going to do tomorrow?" I try to link things as much as possible.

Background

Marisa is an extremely talented young teacher. Since obtaining her teaching credential, she has taught grades 4 and 5 and a combined 4/5 class in an urban school with 50 percent English Language Learners. Most of the ELL students are recent immigrants from Somalia, Ethiopia, Korea, and Eastern Europe. There are some middle-class families in the neighborhood but the school is classified as high needs. Marisa speaks highly of her initial undergraduate degree, a four-year program in Early Childhood Education (infancy through the primary grades) with a strong emphasis on child development and field placements each year. She then attended a two-year teacher credential program at OISE/UT. Although she felt the practicum placements in the latter program did not provide examples of good literacy instruction ("the programs did not have a focus"), she found the university literacy courses valuable. While completing her pre-service program Marisa worked at summer camps, first as a counselor and later in a supervisory position.

For the classroom observations of our study participants, research team members are asked to provide four words they feel best characterize the teaching approach of the new teacher they are observing. One of the researchers described Marisa using the terms *scholarly*, *routines*, *group learning*, and *respect/community*; another saw her as thoughtful, relational, organized, and teaching with a purpose. Yet these terms do not fully capture the essence of Marisa. When observing her, we were continually impressed by the construction of her lessons, each step clearly thought through, all done in a warm, supportive class community. She spends an extraordinary amount of time on lesson planning because she believes that lessons need to build on each other in line with a conception of where the program is headed.

Vision for her literacy program

In her third year of teaching, Marisa described her vision for literacy teaching as follows:

> I want to teach students a variety of strategies for reading a variety of texts. I want them to be able to talk about what they are reading and know that, for example, when you're reading non-fiction there are several components to it. I want them to know the proper terms and be able to talk about them, explain how they are used, and use them.

I want them to enjoy reading but I also want them to talk about books and really understand them. In terms of writing, I hope they will see writing as something they can have fun with. I know I wasn't raised that way. I want them to see writing as something that is free, you can choose whatever writing form you want, you can express ideas, it's up to you.

Marisa's vision may be elaborated in terms of four aspects of her work.

Sequencing the program

Marisa feels that one of the challenges of teaching is knowing when to teach a particular topic or concept, and she believes she must choose the order of topics and skills based on the research on how children learn. When teaching mathematics she knows that you must teach skip counting before multiplication, yet she feels there is not the same certainty regarding literacy. Working with her mentor, grade team, and in-school literacy coordinator, Marisa has developed a well-sequenced program. She refers to the research literature and continually tries to balance short-term and long-term goals. She said:

> I am not teaching character traits just because it's fun and that's all I can think of, I am teaching them because next we're going to be focusing on relating to text. It will help kids relate to text better if they can identify and relate to the characters.

She has developed an approach to planning that works for her, conceptualizing her program in six-week blocks: three weeks of reading (e.g., workshop, whole-group instruction, individual reading) followed by three weeks of writing (e.g., workshop, modeled writing, individual and group projects). She has found this system highly effective because it links reading and writing and provides students with sufficient exposure to a concept, genre, or skill before having to incorporate it in their writing. For example, when doing a newspaper unit, she spent a few weeks having the children read and study newspapers, "looking at bias, fact versus opinions, and how newspapers are supposed to be based on facts." After this intensive study, the students produced a class newspaper.

Engaging the students

Marisa uses a range of teaching techniques and develops interesting end-of-unit projects for students to demonstrate their learning. She carefully chooses topics from the mandated curriculum that are relevant and interesting. For example, she has a poem of the week, word walls for content areas, and debates on topics such as: Have cell phones improved our lives? And she has the class read topical novels such as *The Breadwinners* (there are a number of Muslim students in her class, several of them from Afghanistan). She is well aware that many of her students do not have the same opportunities that children from more advantaged families may have. She addresses this by using videos, going on field trips, incorporating non-fiction texts in the program, and sharing her life experiences with the students.

> They need background knowledge. A reluctant reader or even a struggling reader, if they know a lot about a topic, that will help them understand what they are reading. And so I hope to build that background knowledge and expose them to things that are happening in the world as well.

Being selective and teaching skills for life-long learning

One of the struggles Marisa faces with program planning is the sheer volume of content to be covered. By the end of her first year of teaching she already realized that she could not address all the official expectations:

> I'm starting to learn that, as someone said to me once, there are no curriculum police and no one is really going to know if I teach all the expectations. Anyway, it's unrealistic to assume – especially in a content area – that you can cover everything. And why would I want to?

She does not want to simply "cover the curriculum"; rather she aims to teach skills, ones that students can apply in their own reading and writing and that will stay with them. In her third year, she said:

> I'm getting better at choosing what's important. That's debatable, because what one person thinks is important another person might have a different opinion about. What I try to do is focus on the skills involved, the bigger concepts, and not just the facts, particularly in science and social studies. I know they will forget the facts a few years from now. I try to use science and social studies as a vehicle to teach skills, like making observations, applying what you know to the outside world, and building background knowledge.

Whenever possible she makes links with the students' lives, teaching skills they can use beyond the classroom. For example,

> a lot of our kids love being on the internet, they are very adept at surfing the net, and they're motivated. But they need to be taught how to use it effectively in terms of doing research. Or they need to be taught how to use it safely or critically.

She incorporates these skills into her content area teaching; for example, which search engines help you when researching a specific topic such as popular music.

Building a strong community

One of the foundational pieces of Marisa's vision is for the class to become a learning community. Her success in achieving this is evident in the way the children talk to each other and work together. She uses many of the strategies she learned in the Tribes training she completed while being a student teacher. She talks to the students about their community, helping them acquire the necessary language and grasp the importance of social skills. She believes that by having a collaborative culture in the class she is able to use many more teaching techniques (e.g., group work, Readers' Theater, debates). She incorporates learning about community into her literacy program.

> A lot of the books for read-alouds were about community. There were books about different kinds of families, different roles, boys versus girls, and issues we dealt with in class. Every time we read a different book, we would talk about, "Okay, what can we learn about building community from this book?" And the kids brainstormed things like "friends should support each other," and "everyone is equal, regardless of the color of their skin."

Marisa's class in action

Marisa's classroom reflects a language-rich environment, with bins of books, word walls, charts, posters, and student work on display. The classroom is old but very tidy and inviting. When Marisa's grade 4 and 5 students enter the class, there is a friendly buzz. They gather on the carpet by the whiteboard to review the characters in the book *Dionella* (a fractured fairy tale). They have been working on different genres of literature and are now studying fairy tales. Marisa forms random groups and each must identify three character traits of a particular character in *Dionella*.

After about 15 minutes, she uses a rain stick to get the students' attention to reconvene on the carpet. She has copied some dialogue from the book on charts, and the students who discussed a particular character have to read the lines in a way that reveals their character. There is lots of laughter and enthusiasm for the task. Marisa uses sophisticated language such as "Add a little more arrogance to your voice" as she gives feedback to the students. The students then work in groups (previously selected by Marisa) to practice their Readers' Theater (based on the same fairy tale) that they will perform later in the week. Again, the groups work very well together, with students assisting each other with the text (the ELL students are mixed into the groups and the grade 4 and 5 students work together).

After recess, the class meets on the carpet for a math lesson. They begin by working with a partner to practice their multiplication facts. After the drill, they have a lesson on doubling (multiplication). Students are attentive and keen. After each student gives his or her answer, Marisa asks for an explanation of the pattern. The students are used to explaining their answers and use correct mathematical language. She then distributes mini-whiteboards and the whole class practices doubling patterns. As the end of the day approaches, the students tidy up and organize their homework. Throughout the day, the environment in the class has been calm and friendly. It is obvious that the children enjoy school and are happy in the class.

Final thoughts

Marisa's vision for teaching was shaped by many factors: her own love of reading and writing, her strong undergraduate program, the emphasis on research in her teacher credential program, the fine mentoring she received, the principal of the school, who is very knowledgeable about literacy teaching, her reading of professional texts, and her induction workshops. She is proud of her program and rightly so. She said she would give the following advice to a new teacher:

> Don't be overwhelmed by all of the resources out there . . . because you can get too caught up with doing things that are fun and having neat lessons. If it doesn't connect back to your overall planning, your overall expectations, and if it doesn't make sense in the sequence of your whole year, then you're wasting your time.

What and why of a vision for teaching

Traditionally the word "vision" has often suggested something rather mysterious or otherworldly. But today it is increasingly used to refer to a working understanding and set of images that guide a teacher (Grossman et al., 2000; Hammerness, 2006). In this vein, Kennedy (2006) says:

> Although I use the term *vision* to describe teachers' plans, I do not mean this in the religious, idealist, or head-in-the-clouds sense of the term but rather, to mean that teachers have a feet-on-the-ground sense of purpose and direction and of actions that get there from here. They are plans – not plans that are developed in a logical or rational way but scenarios that are envisioned.

(p. 207)

An envisioned plan of this kind is sometimes called a philosophy of teaching or an approach to teaching, and there is considerable merit in these terms. Certainly a comprehensive philosophy or body of theory is crucial to effective teaching, and some may feel this is safer terminology. But the word vision has additional connotations that are important. It points to components such as vivid images of practice and emotional commitment on the part of the teacher (Hammerness, 2006). A vision is more obviously something a teacher can be passionate about. Nevertheless, *we would not insist on this particular word*: what matters is that we have something like a vision, whatever terminology we decide to use.

A vision should be distinguished from a mission or vision *statement*. Roland Barth (2004) illustrates the problem of confusing the two:

Roland: Does your school have a vision?
Teacher: Oh, yes.
Roland: Could you tell me what it is?
Teacher: I can't get all the words straight . . . they have it down at the office.

(p. 194)

Whereas a vision statement is explicit, a vision for teaching may be mainly implicit (Newman, 1990). Further, a vision statement is typically brief and very general, whereas a well-developed vision for teaching is a vast network of general, medium-grain, and specific components. A vision statement could conceivably be developed at a weekend retreat, but our vision for teaching has been forming since well before we began our credential program and will continue to grow in major ways throughout our career.

Not only is a teaching vision extensive, it is also flexible and changeable. Some people worry that having a vision for teaching will unduly constrain our choices. But although a vision does point us in certain directions, we are free to act differently in a given situation and then perhaps modify the vision in light of the outcome. Our vision should always be seen as a work in progress, otherwise experimentation and gaining of new insights will be hindered.

There are several reasons for teachers to have a well-developed vision. First, a vision keeps us aware of *the full range of goals and processes of teaching*. Sometimes in schooling we have become too narrow in our concerns. Teaching has long been bedeviled by fads, bandwagons, and pendulum swings that suggest we have at last found "the answer." By contrast, a vision makes clear from the outset that many factors are involved in effective teaching. For example, even the highly valuable "teaching for understanding" movement in education, spear-headed by the National Council of Teachers of Mathematics and National Council of Teachers of English (Beck, Hart, and Kosnik, 2002; Zemelman, Daniels, and Hyde,

1998), has tended to focus too much on one aspect of teaching, namely, fostering subject knowledge. Many years ago, Goodlad (1966) pointed to the dangers of basing schooling just on the study of academic disciplines. Similarly, Noddings (2005) questions the value of schooling that is preoccupied with "liberal education," that is, studying arts and science subjects, to the neglect of what she calls the "caring" aspects of life. Recently, "multiliteracies" advocates (Cope and Kalantzis, 2000; New London Group, 1996) have argued that we must have a broad view of the goals and processes of schooling, linking them to students' life and literacies beyond the school. Having a comprehensive vision of teaching can help us keep this broad perspective.

Second, a vision helps us see *how the various aspects of teaching fit together*. This is necessary, on the one hand, so we can address inconsistencies and conflicts in our goals and practices. Kennedy (2006) notes that the aims society has for teaching are "inconsistent with one another"; for example, there is

> a tension between the desire to follow students' interests and the desire to ensure that required content is covered . . . between the desire to develop children as ethically and socially responsible human beings and the desire to endow them with the skills they need to find employment.
>
> (p. 206)

She maintains that teacher educators must foster in student teachers a vision that enables them to deal with such tensions. On the other hand, even where the goals of teaching do not conflict, we need a vision that integrates them and enables us to pursue them simultaneously. This is necessary both to save time and so our teaching activities reinforce each other.

Third, having an explicit vision is important so teachers can *explain to students the purposes of schooling and particular classroom practices*. This increases students' motivation, encourages them to take ownership of their learning, and helps them become life-long learners. It also improves the teacher–student relationship and general classroom climate as students see that their teacher is not just making arbitrary demands but is working in a caring and purposeful manner to meet their needs. Even where students do not fully understand or accept a teacher's explanation, they usually appreciate the respect shown by trying to provide one. Carrie, one of the new teachers in our study, noted that she attempts to explain various aspects of school life to her grade 8 students:

> I talk a lot about *why*. Like even with the student dress-code: does anyone have any idea why we ask you not to wear a hat in class? And I try to explain why I feel the way I do about it. I find they buy into it

more, and are more willing to go along with things. And even, why are we studying Shakespeare?

Problems of a vision for teaching

Although it is important for teachers to have a vision, there are a number of potential challenges in this area. One is that the visions presented in books and programs on teaching are often too *abstract*. Some new teachers (unlike most of our study participants) largely dismiss the theory aspect of their pre-service program because of its generality; they feel that only in practice teaching did they learn the "nuts and bolts" of how to teach. The abstract nature of much educational theory is often due to the fact that it is developed by professors who lack current contact with schools. But it also arises in part from the view held by some academics that they can single-handedly produce useful theory: solutions are developed at a theoretical level and then "trickle down" to the practitioners below. We think this view must be rejected. Sound educational theory can be developed only by people who are in touch with the realities of the classroom (Carr, 1995; Dewey, 1916). This means that theorists must spend a lot of time in the field or at least work very closely with practitioners and field-based researchers in developing a vision for teaching.

Another problem is that visions for teaching are often too *narrow*. The main focus is on transmission by teachers of "school knowledge," with little attention to the needs of work, citizenship, or personal and social growth. Meier (1995) speaks about how certain school subjects such as science and mathematics have been privileged by our conception of an educated person, while other areas such as the arts – which may in fact be more important for personal fulfillment and even career success – are barely on the radar. Kennedy (2006) notes that although teaching is a complex activity with many "areas of concern," unfortunately "[m]ost of the advice teachers get from others does not address all these things" (pp. 205–206).

Visions for teaching are also frequently *unrealistic*. This may arise from lack of practical knowledge on the part of the theorists who develop them, as noted above; but it may also arise from political factors. Politicians and education officials tend to heap more and more responsibilities on teachers to satisfy various constituencies. Schools are represented as "healers of society's woes" (Kosnik, 1999, p. 45) in order to create the impression that the woes are actually being addressed and at remarkably low cost. Berliner and Biddle (1995) and Darling-Hammond (1997) describe how schools are asked to bring about improvements in student learning that are simply not feasible with available levels of financial and other support.

Often visions for teaching are too *fragmented*. Their components are realistic in a sense but they cannot be implemented in isolation. For example, the ideal of "engaging" students (and so having them become "life-long learners") may be unattainable because the curriculum is not related to students' interests. Or the goal of enhancing student self-esteem may not be feasible because the testing and reporting system requires that every child excel in the same way. Or good classroom management may be impossible because not enough emphasis is placed on class community and the teacher–student relationship.

A final problem is that visions for teaching are sometimes seen as *just a matter of opinion*. This may arise because of relativisitic approaches to values or mistaken interpretations of constructivism and other progressive positions. In opposition to this view, and as discussed in the Introduction, we believe the time has come for teacher educators (and others) to take a stand on priorities for teaching. We need to recognize that some visions for teaching are better than others and make a case for the ones we regard as better. Although we should not impose a vision on student teachers, we should work closely and interactively with them to develop a vision that is maximally helpful to pupils. Each teacher must arrive at a distinctive vision, suited to their particular style, interests, talents, and context. But the position they adopt should be a reasonable response to relevant factors rather than an arbitrary, subjective opting for one vision over another.

Key elements of a vision for teaching

In this section, we discuss nine principles that we think are vital to a sound vision for teaching. As in previous chapters we draw on the views and practices of the new teachers in our study, along with other sources. The principles highlighted have all been mentioned before in the book; we address them here to help in exploring the nature and role of a vision for teaching.

A vision for teaching, as noted earlier, is a vast network of ideas, principles, and images touching on both theory and practice. The principles discussed below represent just a small proportion of a teaching vision. However, they are principles that are frequently neglected in schooling and so serve to illustrate how having a vision can make a difference. In our view, if these principles were widely implemented, the school today (indeed the world) would be a much better place.

These nine principles, though fairly general, are still medium-grain in nature. Underlying them are a handful of even more basic principles, notably: an inquiry approach to teaching; student construction of knowledge; interactive or reciprocal teaching; and individualization of teaching. We will often refer to these basic principles in our discussion since they are essential to our vision for teaching; however, they will not be our main focus here because we wish to work at a more concrete level. The principles we will use in illustrating a vision for teaching are:

1. pursuing a broad range of goals
2. selecting and prioritizing objectives, topics, and activities
3. connecting to students' lives
4. engaging students
5. teaching for depth
6. integrating learning
7. building community in the classroom
8. teaching inclusively
9. building a close teacher–student relationship.

As we consider the above principles, we suggest pondering questions such as the following:

*   How much positive difference would implementing this set of principles make?
*   How important is it, then, to have a vision for teaching?
*   How important is it to articulate such principles explicitly?

Pursuing a broad range of goals

As we teach, we should pursue multiple purposes for our students. These include not only subject knowledge and general cognitive development but also social, emotional, aesthetic, moral, behavioral, and other forms of growth. Schooling today in many countries occupies a great deal of young people's lives – 12, 14, or even 18 years (if we include kindergarten and undergraduate university). In many ways schooling *is* their life for a fifth to a quarter of their time on the planet. Given this, a narrow academic focus is unacceptable, whether from the point of view of present quality of life or of preparation for the future. The "multiliteracies" of school, home, local community, workplace, and popular culture must all be addressed (Cope and Kalantzis, 2000; New London Group, 1996).

All the new teachers we studied were aware, in varying degrees, of the need for a broad set of teaching goals. For example, Karen commented:

> I want to have fun and I want the kids to have fun too. It's important that they're not just learning facts but learning social skills, how to treat each other, how to talk about their feelings . . . and developing empathy. That's more important than just facts.

Marisa emphasized attending to ICT in school: "The kids are in the information age, a lot of them love being on the internet." Paul noted that he uses graphic novels in his teaching because having images to look at increases student motivation; he also chooses books geared to his students' interests. In general, Paul believes that:

Having good social relationships is really important, and if kids leave my class with a good sense of citizenship, responsibility, and independence, knowing how to get along with people, taking pride in their work, that is what I want. I want them to learn reading strategies too, but they can only learn them if they have the right attitudes to approach them.

Selecting and prioritizing objectives, topics, and activities

We need a broad set of goals; however, we should not try to cover everything. We must select and prioritize objectives, topics studied, and learning activities. Some goals are more important than others; and besides, no matter how worthy various goals may be, if we cover too many topics our teaching will be superficial. Teachers are under a great deal of pressure today to teach every part of an extremely detailed official curriculum. To fulfill our employment mandate in the current climate it may be necessary to *touch on* a great many topics, but we should make choices about which topics to address thoroughly. This assumes, once again, that we have a clear vision of the purposes we are seeking to achieve.

Most of the teachers in our study had a strong sense of the need to select and prioritize. Even in his first year, David noted that teachers should decide what *they* want to achieve in literacy teaching. Serena observed that a lot of what she does in her class is tailored to what her students need. John commented:

> With my class this year, their reading was very strong but their writing was a big concern, so I focused a lot more on writing . . . Is that appropriate? I think so, because if something is lacking, why should you spread your time across everything? . . . A strength of a teacher is to be able to allocate different timelines to what needs to be covered.

Felicity in her third year said: "I may not get to everything, and in fact if you have a split grade that's impossible. But I'm getting better at focusing on the big ideas." Also in her third year, Wanda reported: "I'm more concerned [now] about making sure the kids have a solid knowledge base in each of the subject areas, rather than hitting all 250 or 300 specific curriculum expectations."

Connecting to students' lives

Among the goals in a sound vision for teaching, we believe, are ones that relate to students' way of life: present and future, in the school and beyond (again, the "multiliteracies" concern). The "usefulness" of learning is a key theme in writing on constructivist learning. According to Piaget, learners "construct ways to make sense of experiences and will continue to use these constructions as long as they work" (Vadeboncoeur, 1997, p. 23). However, schooling must be useful in a broad sense that includes not only students' future career but many other aspects of life as well. Students may not always understand the usefulness of what they are learning, but we should try to help them see it as much as possible and regularly seek feedback from them about how to make their learning more worthwhile. The more they can grasp the links of schooling to life the more they will take ownership of their learning and become life-long learners.

If students are to connect school learning to life they must become self-conscious about developing a way of life. Too often young people (and adults, for that matter) see their way of life as a given rather than something they can create or at least fine-tune. A major aspect of our vision for teaching should be supporting students in consciously forming a way of life, including deciding in what ways to retain the way of life of their family and local community, as discussed in Chapter 4. In today's school systems not much time is available specifically for reflection of this kind, but it can be integrated to a significant degree into subject learning and various classroom activities.

Many of the new teachers we studied stressed the need to connect to students' everyday lives, both present and future. Sophia reported that although in a sense she prepares students for standardized tests, her main concern is to give them "strategies for life . . . strategies they will not only be using for test writing but also in life, to figure out solutions to problems." Carrie noted: "I talk a lot about what adults do in different jobs [and relate it to their studies]: why would you need to know how to do this? Why is it important?" Paul commented:

> I want them to get used to seeing reading as something they're always doing; not just books but the newspaper, emails, street signs, labels on products. They're always reading, but a lot of them think reading is when you get this long book with chapters and have to read it endlessly, and they just hate that.

Anita said that:

> part of my vision is that students leave with the idea that, over the years, their knowledge will increase constantly . . . Students say, "Oh but I know this, we did it last year," and I say, "Well, this is a new year. Your knowledge is going to keep changing as you get older, that's what happens when we mature."

Engaging students

Students will not always enjoy their learning, even when it is clearly important to them. But the high degree of alienation from school work often found among students today is unacceptable. It results in inefficient learning and often prejudices students against certain areas and types of learning for the rest of their lives. Policy makers, curriculum developers, and teachers need to do more to ensure that the topics and activities selected are interesting and valuable to students, and teachers should try to bring students on board by giving them more choice and systematically explaining to them the value of what they are studying.

The engagement of students is necessary if they are to genuinely "inquire" into subjects and join in constructing knowledge, as is widely advocated today. Engagement in turn requires a high degree of individualization of instruction: students vary in what they are capable of and find engaging. As we saw in Chapter 1, the teachers in our study were initially shocked at the academic diversity in their classes and had to scramble to find ways to address it. Although individualizing teaching will always be a challenge, we believe new teachers should come from pre-service viewing individualized instruction as *the norm* and already armed with strategies for doing it, to the extent feasible.

All the teachers in our study spoke of the importance of engaging students and attending to their individual needs and interests. Wanda stressed getting to know students so you can choose appropriate books for them and find "the big hook that's going to draw the child in. Because if the child is not engaged they're not going to learn, they'll just turn you off." Paul suggested that often when students are seen as having a learning disability, the main problem is in fact lack of engagement:

> The first thing I want to do is get the students excited and interested. Because although some of them have specific needs or disabilities, for the most part they just need to get connected to something they're really excited about. So for some students, letting them read something that maybe isn't at their grade level but that they're interested in – a newspaper, something on the internet, a recipe book, or whatever – will get them reading.

Jeannie noted the importance of student choice:

> I like the idea of students writing on a topic of their choice; whereas when I was in school it was more prescribed . . . I used to be against free choice, thinking that they probably don't do much on the weekend other than sit in their apartment playing video games, and how are they going to write about that? But most of them come up with pretty good things. Even though they may talk a lot about going to Wal-Mart,

each time they go it's with someone different, or they buy something different, or they're feeling different, like they're upset because they didn't get to buy something. I have found giving them choice is really successful.

Felicity commented: "I don't torture the kids with weekly grammar lessons. I think things have changed [since I went to school]: the kids need to be excited about writing, they need a focus for their writing, they need an audience for their writing."

Teaching for depth

As discussed in Chapter 5, subject matter learning is of course very important. However, it is only valuable if it goes beyond superficial memorization of "facts" to grasping key concepts and issues in depth. Many aspects of the vision for teaching we have discussed so far relate to this point. For example, selecting and prioritizing are necessary so that we can focus in depth on a smaller number of crucial topics. And engaging students and connecting to their lives leads to their inquiring into topics more deeply and understanding them more fully.

Depth should not be understood just in academic terms. Subject specialists sometimes lay out an ambitious program of disciplinary learning that in fact leaves little room for deeper study of life issues. A student may have a lot of knowledge of history, for example, but only a superficial grasp of related dimensions of life such as politics, social relationships, and human well-being. Seeing the implications of a historical phenomenon for everyday life is an important aspect of understanding it deeply.

Among the new teachers in our study, many spoke of the need to teach in depth. Maria commented:

[In literacy] we should focus more on higher order thinking, questions of how to inference, how to do things that as adults we do all the time but don't remember learning: the skills that are going to get you through. Being able to inference is a higher kind of intelligence than, let's say, being able to re-tell a story . . . We spend way too much time in school on re-telling.

Anita reported that her goal in literacy teaching "is to have the kids be able to understand what they're reading, talk about it, think about it critically, and then express their thoughts . . . in a clear, organized way so other people can read them." Liane noted:

A concern I've had about my program in the past is not having time to go deeply into anything. I've felt I'm just touching on things: floating around and not achieving anything great. So this year I really slowed down. I wanted to spend a lot of time making it great: working on introductions, arguments, how to conclude . . . [A]nd it paid off; some of their essays were fabulous.

Tanya said that in teaching reading we should spend more time on "comprehension strategies" rather than being content with children just "sounding it out."

Integrating learning

Integration of learning is another important aspect of a vision for teaching. Integrating subjects and topics helps engage students as they see what they are learning in context rather than as just one more thing to cover. It fosters genuine inquiry and knowledge construction by students. It makes learning deeper as students grasp the underlying principles and the connections between subjects. It enables us to address many different topics at once, thus freeing up time to pursue issues in depth. It makes learning more useful, because in the "real world" most problems cut across discipline lines. And it enables us to teach in a more holistic manner as we deal with cognitive, social, and emotional learning together, e.g., literature and the arts, history and literature, science and politics.

As indicated in Chapter 1, many of the new teachers had a strong sense of the need to integrate learning. For example, several noted that integrating the learning of spelling and grammar into literacy activities was more effective than approaching them separately. According to Anita, in teaching spelling and grammar "the key thing is to not just talk about something once but rather to show its importance by bringing it up again and again . . . showing its value by modeling and making it stand out. That way they tend to remember it." Sophia reported:

> I try to integrate math with other subjects. Right now I'm doing probability in math, and I link that with prediction in reading, because probability is about being able to predict what's going to happen next . . . And we're also doing medieval times at present, and I connect work on historical time-lines with the study of math and time.

Building community in the classroom

Building a strong class community – with the teacher as a member – must be a central component of our vision for teaching. Traditionally the teacher has tended to be viewed as transmitting knowledge to a collection of students whose interactions with each other should be kept to a minimum so they can concentrate on the material and absorb it (Peterson, 1992). But if this is our primary image, our success as teachers will be limited. Class community supports the *social* construction of knowledge that is increasingly emphasized today (Beck and Kosnik, 2006; Richardson, 1997). It enables us to achieve some of the broader goals of teaching, such as social skills and understanding of human nature and interactions. It links the classroom to the "multiliteracies" of the outside world as students share aspects of their home and local community life. Class community results in students becoming more engaged in inquiry: because they know each other, they are more willing to participate and say what they think in small-group and whole-class settings. It also reduces classroom management problems, thus leaving more time for teaching in depth.

As we saw in Chapter 3, building community in the classroom was a major aspect of the vision for teaching articulated by the new teachers in our study. For example, John stressed the importance of students sharing with each other and feeling safe and relaxed in the classroom. Paul reported:

> I spent a lot of time at the beginning of the year on cooperative work because I found that although these students are very sweet, they didn't seem to have a lot of motivation to work together, to help each other, to watch out for each other.

Maria said:

> [W]e do a lot of discussion in class . . . And they are not necessarily good at that: I mean, kids often don't know how to have a conversation . . . Since the first day of school, I've been drilling them about manners, even just when someone greets you "Hi, how are you today?" you ask the person back, "I'm fine thanks, how are you?"

Tanya commented:

> I've worked hard on having a very helpful [classroom] environment, and especially having the students help each other. We've done a lot of talking about, okay, you have a problem, before you come to me what are you going to do to try to solve it? The main goal is cooperation and class community.

Teaching inclusively

As discussed in Chapter 4, taking account of the diverse backgrounds and abilities of students is essential to connecting to their lives, engaging them, building class community, and many other aspects of the teacher's role. Teaching inclusively should not be viewed as a frill or just the politically correct thing to do, but as a fundamental dimension of sound teaching. Inclusion is inherent in a "multiple teaching" approach that respects students' circumstances, talents, and experiences and seeks to enlist them in constructing knowledge.

Many of the new teachers in our study reported that inclusion was an important part of their vision for teaching. Sophia stressed attending to "the different cultures and background experiences of all the students." John spoke about the need to "tailor [your program] to the students you're teaching," and gave an example:

> [W]e made a quilt . . . Not a lot of kids in my class celebrate Christmas, so I said "Well, for each square of this quilt, I want you to write about a special occasion in your religion for the year. So a lot of the kids wrote about Chinese New Year, a lot about Eids, that type of thing as well as Christmas. So I was able to bring us all together to hold hands as a group, I guess, and put it together on a quilt that I've hung outside my classroom.

Sophia tries to integrate her ELL students as much as possible into the class, and finds that implementing a multiple intelligences philosophy benefits them, along with the other students.

Building a close teacher–student relationship

A close teacher–student relationship is basic to all other aspects of a sound vision for teaching. Pursuing diverse goals, prioritizing topics and activities, engaging students, teaching for depth, and integrating learning depend on the teacher having knowledge of students' individual interests, abilities, and needs. Community building and inclusion require modeling by the teacher of a caring, respectful relationship with each student. Connecting to students' lives is such a sensitive task that it is not feasible unless teachers know their students well and have a positive rapport with them.

Many of the new teachers we interviewed emphasized the teacher–student relationship. Paul spoke of the need to model good relationships:

> You have to be so patient with kids who are acting up all the time, because if you react in a very angry way, that's what they see and how they'll react to each other. I think my students have learned a lot from me about how you get someone to respond to you. You have to be polite; if you just order people around, they're not going to listen to you.

Later Paul observed: "A lot of stuff I do with the students is just talking to them, heart to heart, trying to bring out their humanity, looking them

in the eye . . . [As] opposed to just, okay, you're suspended, off you go."
Heather, who is a special education teacher, noted that the benefit of working one-on-one with students is that "you get to know them so well [and]
that makes a huge difference." Anna commented:

> [W]here I've connected most with the students is just the chats, their
> coming to me when they have a problem. Not necessarily academic –
> though they like the way I explain things to them several times and so
> on. But it's more how I connect to them. They feel I'm not just an adult
> in the classroom but somebody they can talk to.

And Vera, looking back at the end of her third year, said:

> I don't think my ideals have changed . . . but I do find myself enjoying
> the kids' company a lot more. In my first year, I was mainly concerned
> about keeping them busy, and now my concern is more talking to them,
> getting to know them, learning about how they learn, and then using
> that to teach them.

Implications for pre-service education

We have suggested that having a vision for teaching should be a priority in
teacher education. How can we move in this direction? The following are
just a few of the main implications of this priority for pre-service preparation.

Vision for teaching should be constantly discussed with student teachers

Many very specific matters are addressed in pre-service preparation, and
this needs to be balanced by discussion of overall goals and principles that
give direction to teaching and ensure that the various components support
(rather than undermine) each other. Some student teachers may resist such
discussion, describing it as too academic or "airy fairy" and objecting that
they "came here to learn how to teach," not to discuss vague generalities.
We should not dismiss these concerns, but rather try to win over these
students by illustrating general principles with concrete examples, showing
that sound theory is in fact essential for effective teaching.

In these discussions, the term *vision* should not be insisted on: people
often prefer other terms such as philosophy, approach, pedagogy, or theory.
The same term has different connotations for different people, and it is
the concept rather than the term that is important. Further, we should not
insist that all student teachers adopt the same vision. On the contrary, they
should be encouraged to develop a vision that is tailored to their distinctive

needs, talents, circumstances, and outlook, while also meeting the needs of their students. Only in this way will they take ownership of the exploration, think deeply about the topic, and come up with helpful insights about directions for teaching.

The faculty team should often discuss vision for teaching

As with the student teachers, we should not aim at having all faculty adopt the same vision: allowing divergence, once again, fosters ownership and insight. However, faculty should be encouraged to *have* a comprehensive vision, and be given opportunities in meetings, at retreats, and in other contexts to learn from each other and deepen and expand their vision. Pre-service faculty typically have similar views on many matters (Kennedy, 2006), and these common ideas need to be articulated and refined and additional issues tackled. A statement of "what our program stands for" should be developed to provide initial guidance to students and new faculty, but again with the understanding that not all faculty or students may fully agree and that these matters are open to ongoing exploration and revision. To the extent that the faculty agree on elements of a vision for teaching, further discussion is needed of how these elements will be addressed in the program.

The breadth and integration of a vision should be stressed

In keeping with our earlier discussion of the nature of a vision for teaching, the vast extent and interconnectedness of a vision should be emphasized in the pre-service program. In this chapter we outlined nine elements that we regard as essential to a vision for teaching, but these were by way of illustration; many more could have been mentioned. Because pupils are in the school's care for such a long time, there are many goals and principles that teachers must bear in mind in order to teach well. Moreover, the goals range from teaching academics to helping pupils function well in the various settings of life, both now and in the future.

If such a broad agenda is to be fulfilled, economies of time and effort must be achieved by integration of teaching activities. Pupils must learn how to cooperate *as* they learn how to read and write; they must learn to relate to adults *as* they discuss academic matters with their teachers; they must learn about politics *as* they learn historical facts. Fortunately, integrating learning in this way happens to be the most effective way to learn in many cases. The vision for teaching we introduce to our student teachers, then, should be one not of pursuing a number of priorities in isolation, but of developing learning activities in which many priorities are achieved at once.

Conclusion

In order to make sound decisions about what and how to teach, teachers need a comprehensive, integrated understanding of the goals, principles, and practices of teaching. Because of its distinctive connotations, the word *vision* is increasingly being used to refer to this understanding. But the particular term is not crucial: it could equally be called a philosophy or theory of teaching or an approach to teaching. The main point is that it pulls together all the other priorities, keeping teachers aware of the enormous range of considerations involved in teaching, including the extensive links to personal life and "the real world."

In pre-service education, we have sometimes neglected fostering vision in student teachers, instead providing endless strategies, activities, practical tips, and information about curriculum documents and learning materials. At other times we have attempted to address vision, but our proposals have been abstract, overly idealistic, and fragmented – even inconsistent. What we need to do is help student teachers develop a vision for teaching that is theoretical yet concrete, idealistic yet realistic, and comprehensive yet selective and integrated. This is a tall order, of course. But new teachers are faced immediately with having to cobble together a viable teaching approach if they are to teach well and survive in the profession. It is inappropriate for them to have to do this largely on their own. We must ensure that the work of developing a vision for teaching is begun in a major way during the pre-service program.

References

Ainscow, M., Booth, T., and Dyson, A. (2006). *Improving schools, developing inclusion*. London: Routledge.

Allington, R. (2006). *What really matters for struggling readers: Designing research-based programs* (2nd ed.). Boston: Pearson/Allyn & Bacon.

Atwell, N. (1998). *In the middle* (2nd ed.). Portsmouth, NH: Heinemann.

Bainbridge, J., and Malicky, G. (2004). *Constructing meaning: Balancing elementary language arts* (3rd edn.). Toronto: Thomson/Nelson.

Ball, D. (2000). Bridging practices: Intertwining content and pedagogy in teaching and learning to teach. *Journal of Teacher Education, 51*(3), 241–247.

Barone, D., and Morrow, L. M. (eds.) (2003). *Literacy and young children: Research-based practices*. New York: Guilford Press.

Barth, R. (1990). *Improving schools from within*. San Francisco: Jossey-Bass.

Barth, R. (2004). *Learning by heart*. San Francisco: Jossey-Bass.

Barton, D., and Hamilton, M. (1998). *Local literacies: Reading and writing in one community*. London: Routledge.

Beck, C., Hart, D., and Kosnik, C. (2002). The teaching standards movement and current teaching practices. *Canadian Journal of Education, 27*(2), 153–172.

Beck, C. and Kosnik, C. (2001). From cohort to community in a pre-service teacher education program. *Teaching and Teacher Education, 17*, 925–948.

Beck, C., and Kosnik, C. (2006). *Innovations in teacher education: A social constructivist approach*. Albany, NY: SUNY Press.

Berliner, D., and Biddle, B. (1995). *The manufactured crisis*. Reading, MA: Addison-Wesley.

Bransford, J., Darling-Hammond, L., and LePage, P. (2005). Introduction. In L. Darling-Hammond and J. Bransford (eds.), *Preparing teachers for a changing world: What teachers should learn and be able to do* (pp. 1–39). San Francisco: Jossey-Bass.

Calderhead, J., and Shorrock, S. (1997). *Understanding teacher education: Case studies in the professional development of beginning teachers*. London: Falmer.

Cappello, M., and Farnan, N. (2006). Teacher preparation programs situate school curricula in the larger context of teaching and learning. In S. D. Lenski, D. Grisham, and L. Wold (Eds.), *Literacy teacher preparation: Ten truths teacher educators need to know*. Newark, DE: International Reading Association.

Carr, W. (1995). *For education: Towards critical educational inquiry*. Buckingham: Open University Press.

Clayton, C. (2007). Curriculum making as novice professional development: Practical risk taking as learning in high-stakes times. *Journal of Teacher Education, 58*(3), 216–230.

Cochran-Smith, M., Davis, D., and Fries, K. (2004). Multicultural teacher education: Research, practice, and policy. In J. Banks and C. McGee Banks (Eds.), *Handbook of research on multicultural education* (2nd ed.) (pp. 931–975). San Francisco: Jossey-Bass.

Cochran-Smith, M., and Lytle, S. (1993). *Inside/outside: Teacher research and knowledge.* New York: TC Press.

Connelly, M., and Clandinin, J. (1999). *Shaping a professional identity: Stories of educational practice.* New York: Teachers College Press.

Cope, B., and Kalantzis, M. (Eds.) (2000). *Multiliteracies: Literacy learning and the design of social futures.* London: Routledge.

Cossey, R., and Tucher, P. (2005). Teaching to collaborate, collaborating to teach. In L. Kroll, R. Cossey, D. Donahue, T. Calguera, V. LaBoskey, A. Richert, and P. Tucher, *Teaching as principled practice: Managing complexity for social justice* (pp. 105–120). Thousand Oaks, CA: Sage.

Cunningham, P., and Allington, R. (2007). *Classrooms that work: They can all read and write* (4th ed.). Boston: Pearson/Allyn & Bacon.

Danielewicz, J. (2001). *Teaching selves: Identity, pedagogy, and teacher education.* Albany, NY: SUNY Press.

Darling-Hammond, L. (1997). *The right to learn.* San Francisco: Jossey-Bass.

Darling-Hammond, L. (Ed.) (2000). *Studies of excellence in teacher education: Preparation at the graduate level.* Washington, DC: AACTE.

Darling-Hammond, L. (2002). Learning to teach for social justice. In L. Darling-Hammond, J. French, and S. P. Garcia-Lopez (eds.), *Learning to teach for social justice* (pp. 1–7). New York: Teachers College Press.

Darling-Hammond, L. (2006). *Powerful teacher education: Lessons from exemplary programs.* San Francisco: Jossey-Bass.

Darling-Hammond, L., and Bransford, J. (2005). Preface. In L. Darling-Hammond and J. Bransford (Eds.), *Preparing teachers for a changing world: What teachers should learn and be able to do* (pp. vii–x). San Francisco: Jossey-Bass.

Darling-Hammond, L., Ancess, J., and Falk, B. (1995). *Authentic assessment in action: Studies of schools and students at work.* New York: Teachers College Press.

Darling-Hammond, L., Banks, J., Zumwalt, K., Gomez, L., Sherin, M., Griesdorn, J., and Fin, L. (2005). Educational goals and purposes. In L. Darling-Hammond and J. Bransford (eds.), *Preparing teachers for a changing world: What teachers should learn and be able to do* (pp. 169–200). San Francisco: Jossey-Bass.

Delpit, L. (2000). Acquisition of literate discourse: Bowing before the master? In M. Gallego and S. Hollingsworth (Eds.), *What counts as literacy: Challenging the school standard* (pp. 241–251). New York: Teachers College Press.

Dewey, J. (1916). *Democracy and education.* New York: Macmillan.

Dewey, J. (1938). *Experience and education.* New York: Collier-Macmillan.

Edwards, A., and Collison, J. (1996). *Mentoring and developing practice in primary schools: Supporting student teacher learning in schools.* Buckingham: Open University Press.

Evertson, C., Emmer, E., and Worsham, M. (2006). *Classroom management for elementary teachers.* Boston: Pearson.

Falk, B. (2000). *The heart of the matter: Using standards and assessment to learn.* Portsmouth, NH: Heinemann.

Feiman-Nemser, S. (2001). From preparation to practice: Designing a continuum to strengthen and sustain teaching. *Teachers College Record, 103*(6), 1013–1055.

Floden, R., and Buchmann, M. (1990). Coherent programs in teacher education: When are they educational? In *Philosophy of Education 1990* (Proceedings of the Philosophy of Education Society) (pp. 304–314). Normal, IL: PES.

Fountas, I., and Pinnell, G. (2001). *Guiding readers and writers: Teaching comprehension, genre, and content literacy.* Portsmouth, NH: Heinemann.

Freire, P. (1968/72). *Pedagogy of the oppressed.* New York: Herder & Herder.

Gardner, H. (1999). *Intelligence reframed: Multiple intelligences for the 21st century.* New York: Basic Books

Genishi, C. (Ed.) (1992). *Ways of assessing children and curriculum: Stories of early childhood practice.* New York: Teachers College Press.

Gibbs, J. (2000). *Tribes: A new way of learning and being together.* Sausalito, CA: Center Source Systems.

Goodlad, J. (1966). *The changing school curriculum.* New York: Fund for the Advancement of Education.

Goodlad, J. (1990). *Teachers for our nation's schools.* San Francisco: Jossey-Bass.

Goodlad, J. (1994). *Educational renewal: Better teachers, better schools.* San Francisco: Jossey-Bass.

Grossman, P., and Schoenfeld, A. (2005). Teaching subject matter. In L. Darling-Hammond and J. Bransford (Eds.), *Preparing teachers for a changing world: What teachers should learn and be able to do* (pp. 201–231). San Francisco: Jossey-Bass.

Grossman, P., Valencia, S., Evans, K., Thompson, C., Martin, C., and Place, N. (2000). Transitions into teaching: Learning to teach writing in teacher education and beyond. *Journal of Literacy Research, 32*(4), 631–662.

Hagger, H., and McIntyre, D. (2006). *Learning teaching from teachers: Realizing the potential of school-based teacher education.* Maidenhead: Open University Press.

Hammerness, K. (2006). *Seeing through teachers' eyes: Professional ideals and classroom practices.* New York: Teachers College Press.

Hammerness, K., Darling-Hammond, L., and Bransford, J. (2005). How teachers learn and develop. In L. Darling-Hammond and J. Bransford (Eds.), *Preparing teachers for a changing world: What teachers should learn and be able to do* (pp. 390–441). San Francisco: Jossey-Bass.

Hubbard, R., and Power, B. (1993). *The art of classroom inquiry.* Portsmouth, NH: Heinemann.

Irvine, J. (2003). *Educating teachers for diversity: Seeing with a cultural eye.* New York: Teachers College Press.

Jablon, J., Dombro, A., and Dichtelmiller, M. (1999). *The power of observation.* Washington, DC: Teaching Strategies Inc.

Jacklin, A., Griffiths, V., and Robinson, C. (2006). *Beginning primary teaching: Moving beyond survival.* Maidenhead: Open University Press.

Kennedy, M. (2005). *Inside teaching: How classroom life undermines reform.* Cambridge, MA: Harvard University Press.

Kennedy, M. (2006). Knowledge and vision in teaching. *Journal of Teacher Education, 57*(3), 205–211.

Kohn, A. (1999). *The schools our children deserve*. New York: Houghton Mifflin.

Kosnik, C. (1999). *Primary education: Goals, processes, and practices*. Ottawa: Legas.

Kosnik, C. and Beck, C. (2003). The contribution of faculty to community building in a teacher education program: A student teacher perspective. *Teacher Education Quarterly, 30*(3), 99–114.

Labaree, D. (2004). *The trouble with ed schools*. New Haven, CT: Yale University Press.

LeCourt, D. (2004). *Identity matters: Schooling the student body in academic discourse*. Albany, NY: SUNY Press.

LePage, P., Darling-Hammond, L., and Akar, H. (2005). Classroom management. In L. Darling-Hammond and J. Bransford, *Preparing teachers for a changing world: What teachers should learn and be able to do* (pp. 327–357). San Francisco: Jossey-Bass.

Lortie, D. (1975). *Schoolteacher: A sociological study*. Chicago: University of Chicago Press.

Maloch, B., Flint, A. S., Eldridge, D., Harmon, J., Loven, R., Fine, J., Bryant-Shanklin, M. and Martinez, M. (2003). Understandings, beliefs, and reported decision making of first-year teachers from different reading teacher preparation programs. *Elementary School Journal, 103*(5), 431–457.

Martin, J. R. (1992). *The schoolhome*. Cambridge, MA: Harvard University Press.

Meier, D. (1995). *The power of their ideas*. Boston: Beacon Press.

Melnick, S., and Zeichner, K. (1997). Enhancing the capacity of teacher education institutions to address diversity issues. In J. King, E. Hollins, and W. Hayman (Eds.), *Preparing teachers for cultural diversity* (pp. 23–39). New York: Teachers College Press.

Miller, D. (2002). *Reading with meaning: Teaching comprehension in the primary grades*. Markham, ON: Pembroke.

Moll, L., and Gonzalez, N. (2004). Engaging life: A funds-of-knowledge approach to multicultural education. In J. Banks, and C. McGee Banks (Eds.), *Handbook of research on multicultural education* (2nd ed.) (pp. 699–715). San Francisco: Jossey-Bass.

New London Group (1996). A pedagogy of multiliteracies: Designing social futures. *Harvard Educational Review, 66*(1), 6–92.

Newman, J. (1990). *Finding our own way: Teachers exploring their assumptions*. Portsmouth, NH: Heinemann.

Noddings, N. (2005). *The challenge to care in schools: An alternative approach* (2nd ed.). New York: Teachers College Press.

Otero, V. (2006). Moving beyond the "get it or don't" conception of formative assessment. *Journal of Teacher Education, 57*(3), 247–255.

Pahl, K., and Rowsell, J. (2005). *Literacy and education: Understanding the New Literacy Studies in the classroom*. London: Chapman.

Paley, V. (1992). *You can't say you can't play*. Cambridge, MA: Harvard University Press.

Peterson, J., and Hittie, M. (2003). *Inclusive teaching: Creating effective schools for all learners*. Boston: Allyn & Bacon.

Peterson, R. (1992). *Life in a crowded place*. Portsmouth, NH: Heinemann.

Punch, K. (2005). *Introduction to social research: Quantitative and qualitative approaches* (2nd ed.). London: Sage.

Richardson, V. (Ed.) (1997). *Constructivist teacher education: Building a world of new understandings*. London: Falmer.

Roth, R. (ed.) (1999). *The role of the university in the preparation of teachers*. London: Falmer.

Schon, D. (1983). *The reflective practitioner*. New York: Basic Books.

Schoonmaker, F. (2002). *"Growing up" teaching: From personal knowledge to professional practice*. New York: Teachers College Press.

Shepard, L. (1991). The influence of standardized tests on the early childhood curriculum, teachers, and children. In B. Spodek and O. Saracho (Eds.), *Issues in early childhood curriculum: Yearbook in early childhood education, Vol. 2* (pp. 166–189). New York: Teachers College Press.

Shepard, L. (2001). The role of classroom assessment in teaching and learning. In V. Richardson (ed.), *Handbook of research on teaching* (4th ed.) (pp. 1066–1101). Washington, DC: American Educational Research Association.

Shepard, L., Hammerness, K., Darling-Hammond, L., and Rust, F. (2005). Assessment. In L. Darling-Hammond and J. Bransford (Eds.), *Preparing teachers for a changing world: What teachers should learn and be able to do* (pp. 275–326). San Francisco: Jossey-Bass.

Shulman, L. (1986). Those who understand: Knowledge growth in teaching. *Educational Researcher, 15*(2), 4–14. (Also in *The wisdom of practice*, ch. 6, pp. 189–215.)

Shulman, L. (2004). *The wisdom of practice: Essays on teaching, learning, and learning to teach*. San Francisco: Jossey-Bass.

Sleeter, C. (2005). *Un-standardizing curriculum: Multicultural teaching in the standards-based classroom*. New York: TCPress.

Snow, C., Griffin, P., and Burns, M. (2006). *Knowledge to support the teaching of reading: Preparing teachers for a changing world*. San Francisco: Jossey-Bass.

Tom, A. (1997). *Redesigning teacher education*. Albany, NY: SUNY Press.

Vadeboncoeur, J. (1997). Child development and the purpose of education: A historical context for constructivism in teacher education. In V. Richardson (Ed.), *Constructivist teacher education: Building a world of new understandings* (pp. 15–37). London: Falmer.

Vavrus, M. (2002). *Transforming the multicultural education of teachers: Theory, research, and practice*. New York: Teachers College Press.

Verma, G., Bagley, C., and Jha, M. (eds.) (2007). *International perspectives on educational diversity and inclusion*. London: Routledge.

Villegas, A., and Lucas, T. (2002). *Educating culturally responsive teachers: A coherent approach*. Albany, NY: SUNY Press.

Vygotsky, L. (1978). *Mind in society: The development of higher psychological processes*. Cambridge, MA: Harvard University Press.

Wilson, S., Floden, R., and Ferrini-Mundy, J. (2001). *Teacher preparation research: Current knowledge, gaps, and recommendations*. Report prepared for the U.S. Department of Education. Center for the Study of Teaching and Policy: University of Washington.

Wood, G. (1992). *Schools that work*. New York: Penguin/Plume.

Zeichner, K. (1995). Beyond the divide of teacher research and academic research. *Teachers and Teaching: Theory and Practice, 1*(2), 153–172.

Zeichner, K., and Noffke, S. (2001). Practitioner research. In V. Richardson (Ed.), *Handbook of research on teaching* (4th ed.) (pp. 298–332). Washington, DC: American Educational Research Association.

Zemelman, S., Daniels, H., and Hyde, A. (1998). *Best practice*. Portsmouth, NH: Heinemann.

Index